Studying the History of Early English

PERSPECTIVES ON THE ENGLISH LANGUAGE
Series Editor: Lesley Jeffries

Published
Siobhan Chapman Thinking About Language: Theories of English
Urszula Clark Studying Language: English in Action
Christiana Gregoriou English Literary Stylistics
Lesley Jeffries Discovering Language: The Structure of Modern English
Lesley Jeffries Critical Stylistics
Simon Horobin Studying the History of Early English

Forthcoming
Stephen Bax Discourse and Genre
Jonathan Culpeper The Pragmatics of the English Language
Rob Penhallurick Studying Dialect

Perspectives on the English Language Series
Series Standing Order
ISBN 0-333-96146-3 hardback
ISBN 0-333-96147-1 paperback
(outside North America only)

You can receive future titles in this series as they are published by placing a standing order. Please contact your bookseller or, in the case of difficulty, write to us at the address below with your name and address, the title of the series and one of the ISBNs quoted above.

Customer Services Department, Macmillan Distribution Ltd, Houndmills, Basingstoke, Hampshire RG21 6XS, England

Studying the History of Early English

Simon Horobin

palgrave
macmillan

First published 2010 by
PALGRAVE MACMILLAN

Palgrave Macmillan in the UK is an imprint of Macmillan Publishers Limited, registered in England, company number 785998, of Houndmills, Basingstoke, Hampshire RG21 6XS.

Palgrave Macmillan in the US is a division of St Martin's Press LLC, 175 Fifth Avenue, New York, NY 10010.

Palgrave Macmillan is the global academic imprint of the above companies and has companies and representatives throughout the world.

Palgrave® and Macmillan® are registered trademarks in the United States, the United Kingdom, Europe and other countries.

ISBN: 978-0-230-55137-4 hardback
ISBN: 978-0-230-55138-1 paperback

This book is printed on paper suitable for recycling and made from fully managed and sustained forest sources. Logging, pulping and manufacturing processes are expected to conform to the environmental regulations of the country of origin.

A catalogue record for this book is available from the British Library.

A catalog record for this book is available from the Library of Congress.

10 9 8 7 6 5 4 3 2 1
19 18 17 16 15 14 13 12 11 10

Transferred to Digital Printing in 2013

For Jeremy Smith

Contents

Series Editor's Preface   ix
Preface   x

1   Studying Language Change   1
    1.1   Further reading   9

2   Evidence   10
    2.1   Old English   10
    2.2   Early Middle English   15
    2.3   Late Middle English   21
    2.4   Early Modern English   28
    2.5   Further reading   31

3   Standardization   33
    3.1   Old English   35
    3.2   Middle English   36
    3.3   Early Middle English   37
    3.4   Late Middle English   39
    3.5   Early Modern English   47
    3.6   Further reading   51

4   Spellings and Sounds   52
    4.1   Writing systems   52
    4.2   Runes   54
    4.3   Old English   56
    4.4   Middle English   59
    4.5   Early Modern English   63
    4.6   Further reading   71

5   **The Lexicon**   73
     5.1   Word formation   73
     5.2   Old English   75
     5.3   Middle English   77
     5.4   Early Modern English   79
     5.5   Borrowing   82
     5.6   Old English   83
     5.7   Middle English   86
     5.8   Early Modern English   89
     5.9   Semantic change   95
     5.10   Further reading   103

6   **Morphology**   105
     6.1   Nouns   106
     6.2   Determiners   112
     6.3   Adjectives   114
     6.4   Verbs   115
     6.5   Adverbs   120
     6.6   Pronouns   120
     6.7   Further reading   134

7   **Corpus Studies**   135
     7.1   Further reading   144

Bibliography   146
Index   153

Series Editors' Preface

The first three books to be published in the Perspectives on the English Language series (Jeffries, Discovering Language, Chapman, Thinking about Language and Clark, Studying Language) together formed the first wave of what will ultimately be a comprehensive collection of research-based textbooks covering the wide variety of topics in English Language studies. These initial three books provide the basics of English Language description, theory and methodology that students need, whether they are specialists in English Language or taking only one or two modules in the subject. The idea was that these books would be used differently by such different students, and indeed they have already proved useful to postgraduate students as well as undergraduates.

Now we are beginning the process of adding to the series the envisaged set of higher-level textbooks which will build on the core books by bringing together the latest thinking in a range of topics in English Language. This 'second wave' comprises books written by current researchers in the field, and far from simply providing an overview or summary of work so far, these books are distinctive in making the latest research available to a student audience. They are not 'dumbed down', but are written accessibly, with exercises and questions for the reader to consider where relevant. And for the Higher Education teacher, these books provide a resource that s/he can use to bring out the best in students of all abilities.

The book you are holding will ultimately be part of a large series of topic-based books in English Language, and we are confident that you will find them useful and interesting. Although this series was begun with only one series editor, the rate of production of the second wave calls for more help in editing and proofreading. We look forward to surfing this second wave together!

Lesley Jeffries and Dan McIntyre

Preface

This book is not a conventional history of the English language but is intended as a guide to the theoretical and methodological issues that confront students engaged in studying the history of the language. Rather than taking a chronological approach, beginning with Old English and then proceeding to the present day, each chapter is designed to address a specific topic and to consider its relevance to the three major periods in the history of English: Old English, Middle English and Early Modern English. The topics have been selected to give students an insight into a variety of types of linguistic change at different linguistic levels, covering spelling, pronunciation, grammar and lexis. The topics are also intended to emphasize the importance of drawing upon different types of linguistic evidence when attempting to describe and explain linguistic change, including historical, sociolinguistic and philological evidence. Given this orientation readers of this book will benefit from having read a standard narrative account of the history of English, such as can be found in various available publications, several of which are listed in the bibliography at the back of this book, e.g. Barber (1993), Blake (1996) and Baugh and Cable (2001).

In writing this book I have benefited considerably from my experience of teaching the history of the English language in the Department of English Language at the University of Glasgow and in the Faculty of English Language and Literature at the University of Oxford, and I am grateful to my colleagues and students for many interesting discussions of topics covered in this book. In particular, I wish to take this opportunity to thank Professor Jeremy Smith, to whom this book is dedicated, for his unstinting generosity and support throughout my career and for numerous helpful and stimulating conversations which have guided and inspired my work.

Studying Language Change

This book is intended to serve as a handbook for the study of the history of English but, before we look in detail at specific changes in the history of English, I want to consider why languages change and the techniques available for studying these changes, especially changes that occurred in the more distant past. The first point to make is that all living languages are subject to change. The only languages that do not change are dead languages: ones that have no native speakers. We are often made aware of changes happening today by the media who like to lament what they see as the decay of the language. A particular focus of contemporary linguistic prejudice is so-called h-dropping: the omission of initial /h/ from words like *house* and *hand*. People who drop their aitches are traditionally viewed as being ignorant, slovenly and lazy, and the spread of h-dropping is seen as heralding the demise of the English language. Such attitudes are so ingrained in English society that we often fail to stop and wonder why h-dropping should be so frowned upon, and why one pronunciation should be considered better, or more correct, than another. The view that one variety of a language is correct is widespread in English society and is difficult to question. In the first of her BBC Reith lectures of 1996 Jean Aitchison, then Rupert Murdoch Professor of Language and Communication at the University of Oxford, discussed the inevitability of language change and the falsity of many strongly held views about language standards. Her lectures resulted in a postbag full of incensed mail from Radio 4 listeners who objected to her casual attitude towards language variation and her apparent endorsement of certain pronunciations which her listeners considered to be erroneous, such as a pronunciation of kilometre with the stress on the second rather than the first syllable, and the cockney glottal stop, considered by many to be 'the direct result of downright bone idleness' (Aitchison, 2001). Evidently beliefs in correct and incorrect usage run very deep and, despite the fact that the glottal stop requires a tensing of the muscles to produce, it remains stigmatized as a marker of sloppiness and laziness.

Another effect of this belief in correct usage and the importance of upholding linguistic standards is that it creates a resistance to change, which is seen as a lowering of linguistic standards leading to the corruption of the language as a whole. A good example of a change of this kind is the treatment of the word *media* as a singular noun in constructions like 'the media is responsible for corrupting the way we speak'. The reason for this is that *media* is historically the plural form of the Latin noun *medium* and so technically should take a plural verb. So, according to some linguistic pedants, we should say 'the media are responsible for corrupting the way we speak'. According to this view the use of media as a singular noun is simply wrong and should be corrected. When the meaning of a word begins to change many people are often resistant to such change, appealing to the word's 'true' or 'correct' meaning. For instance, many people today use the verb *disinterested* to mean 'not interested' as in 'I'm totally disinterested in this subject' rather than in its other sense 'unprejudiced' or 'unbiased'. Because the sense 'unprejudiced' is more widely accepted it is regarded as correct, while the other usage is regarded as an error prompted by confusion with *uninterested*. However, as the meaning 'uninterested' becomes more widely used and accepted, so this meaning will become the dominant one and will likely replace the sense 'unprejudiced'. Rather than seeing this as a corruption of the language, the replacement of a correct meaning with a false one, we should see this as an example of semantic change, or change in meaning, a topic that we will deal with in greater depth in Chapter 5. One objection that is often raised in response to this kind of argument is that a word's true meaning may be determined by looking at its history, and that an older meaning is more correct than a recent one. But is there really such a thing as a word's true meaning? Appealing to history opens up a whole series of different problems. For many of our English words have long histories and their meanings have changed substantially over time. Take the word *silly* as an example. This word means 'foolish' today, but in Old English it meant 'innocent' or 'blessed'. If we insisted on treating this as the word's true meaning this would lead to all sorts of problems. If we look at the history of the word *disinterested* then we find that the *Oxford English Dictionary* lists two senses:

1. Without interest or concern; not interested, unconcerned;
2. Not influenced by interest; impartial, unbiased, unprejudiced; now always, unbiased by personal interest; free from self-seeking.

Interestingly the first sense is in fact recorded earlier, in 1612, while the second meaning first appears in 1659. So if we were to see the earlier sense as the correct one then we should be using *disinterested* to mean 'without interest' or 'unconcerned'. But appealing to historical dictionaries as arbitrators of present-day usage is artificial, as few people are aware of the etymologies and histories of the words they use, nor do they regularly consult dictionaries or grammars in everyday conversation. A language is, after all, ultimately a means of communication. It makes little difference whether we use alphabets, hieroglyphs, pictograms or runes as long as the message we wish to communicate is understood. The problem with appealing to archaic usages is that they are often no longer understood. If you started using the word *silly* to mean 'innocent' or 'blessed' today, nobody would recognize that this is what you were doing as this meaning is now obsolete, and you would probably find yourselves offending everyone.

Returning to the example of the use of *media* as a singular or plural noun, it is clear that saying 'the media is corrupting the language' does not cause any problems of comprehension. In fact you could argue that in some ways this change is an improvement. A very common feature of English is that noun plurals are typically formed by adding an <-s> to the ends of words: *dog, dogs* and so on, so that having a plural ending in <-a> is an irregularity. Treating *media* as a singular noun makes it accord more neatly with the structure of the language and makes the system more efficient. In fact if we look at this example diachronically, that is through time, then we can see that there has been a general tendency for noun plurals to be regularized to this same paradigm. In Old English there were various noun declensions with a number of different plural endings. The strong masculine noun ending was <-as>, the ancestor of the present-day <-s>, but feminine nouns took <-a> or <-e>, neuters took <-u> or had no ending, while weak nouns had <-n>. Since the OE period many nouns taking <e, a, u, n, Ø> have adopted the more common <-s> ending, creating a more regular and thus more efficient system. The process by which these changes took place will be dealt with in detail in Chapter 6. So, despite the frequency with which people lament changes in the English language, we need to remember that all languages change, and that such changes are not necessarily the result of ignorance and sloppiness. It is not simply the case that older usages are correct and newer innovations are wrong.

Does this mean that the opposite is true: that is, that language change is actually a progression? The example of the noun plurals we have just considered could be used to support such a view. The spread of a single ending produces a more efficient and effective means of communication, ruling out any potential ambiguity and makes it an easier language for children and non-native speakers to learn. When children learn a language they learn both individual words and grammatical rules, so that a child will learn that to form a plural you add <-s> onto a word. This of course leads to some problems, and it is very common to hear young children saying *foots or *sheeps (the asterisk indicates that these are ungrammatical forms). Surely it would be much easier for a child if all nouns behaved the same way, so that *foots and *sheeps became acceptable plural forms? The point of this example is that it shows that while many nouns have adopted the regular <-(e)s> plural form, not all have, even though it would perhaps be 'easier' if they all did. This shows that, just as we need to be wary of talking about language change as a form of corruption, so we need to be careful not to see it as a form of progression. If language change was about creating a leaner and more efficient system, then all such irregularities would have been ironed out so that *foots, *sheeps, *gooses and so on would all be regular features of the language. Returning to our example of *media* we can see that, although this is now typically considered a singular form, there is as yet no corresponding plural form *medias*, although it is possible that such a form will emerge in the future.

A useful metaphor for considering how language change operates is that of evolution, as long as we avoid seeing the history of English as the establishment of a superior and refined standard language from a more primitive ancestor. It is important to remember that Old English, Proto-Germanic and Proto-Indo-European were fully fledged languages, capable of carrying out the communicative tasks required by their speakers, not primitive systems. But if we avoid seeing the history of English as a progression from a less to a more sophisticated system, then the evolutionary model can be a helpful one. After all, the concept of the survival of the fittest is really about adapting best to the current environment, so that giraffes with longer necks will do better in environments where the trees are particularly tall. There is nothing inherently better about having a long neck, and for other animals with different needs, such as those that hide from prey, or need to run fast, or swim, it would be a positive disadvantage. The same is true of languages. There is no reason to prefer the <-s> ending over others, such as <u, n, e> or even <q, x, j> for that matter, it is just that this ending became the one that was selected as the majority variant. Another difference in the noun plural forms between OE and present-day English is that OE had different endings depending upon the function of the noun in the sentence, that is whether it was in the nominative, accusative, genitive or dative case. So the general masculine declension had <-as> for the nominative and accusative cases, but <-a> for the genitive plural and <-um> for the dative plural. As well as the reduction and loss of the various different noun plural endings, the Middle English period also witnessed the simplification and loss of these various case endings so that present-day English retains only the <-s> ending to mark the genitive case. The reduction and loss of these case endings in the noun declensions were part of a widespread process of inflexional simplification and loss that marked the transition from Old to Middle English and saw the language change from being a largely synthetic language, one that relies heavily on inflexions to mark case, number and gender, to a largely analytical language, relying much more on word-order than on endings. You might be tempted to think that the loss of inflexional endings is an example of linguistic progression, the creation of a leaner and more streamlined language system from an unnecessarily cumbersome one. While it is perhaps true that native speakers of present-day English struggle when learning highly inflected languages such as OE or present-day German, this does not necessarily mean that English is a better or easier language. Native speakers of German do not have any difficulty learning their own language, and German has preserved its inflexional system intact over a very long period. Similarly native speakers of OE evidently had no difficulty acquiring the grammatical system of OE, despite its more complex system of inflexion than PDE. The point is that, whether a language relies heavily on inflexional endings, or relies very little on inflexions, does not imply that one is better than the other, both are perfectly adequate means of communication, they are just different. You may be wondering why, if the OE system was perfectly adequate and its speakers had no difficulty acquiring and using it, it does not survive. This is a subject that we will return to in Chapter 6 when we look in detail at the shift from a synthetic to an analytical language.

An important factor in this discussion that we have not yet considered concerns standardization: a topic which forms the subject of Chapter 3. Many languages have a standard variety which is used for important functions, such as in government and the law, and this variety frequently carries social prestige. It is the variety that is generally adopted in the education system and which is taught to children, irrespective of their social or regional background. The function of a standard language is to be understood by the widest possible audience, and so it needs a well-defined and very rigid set of rules. As a result standard languages are particularly intolerant of variation and resistant to change. Let us consider a specific example of this. The English spelling system contains many oddities and irregularities that create unnecessary complications for children and foreign learners, such as silent letters, as in the word *knight*. Surely it would be much more efficient if we simply got rid of these unnecessary letters and simplified the spelling system? As we will see in Chapter 4, these kinds of comments have been made for centuries by people wanting to reform English spelling, many of whom have come up with alternative systems. But none of these systems has ever caught on for the simple reason that standards are fixed varieties that are extremely intolerant of change. If we did start to change the spelling of English, then we would create all sorts of difficulties, especially given that English is now a global language. To retain its usefulness as a means of communication between people all over the world, many of whom are non-native speakers, a relatively fixed variety is needed. A standard language is thus enforced by the education system and by the various institutions that adopt it. If you want to get on in government, or in the law, then you need to use standard English. Thus standard languages inhibit and prevent change. So while children might naturally form non-standard plurals like *foots, parents and teachers will correct them, until they adopt the standard, yet irregular, form *feet*. Standard forms are also reinforced by the written language, so that as children learn to read they are obliged to learn standard spellings. Without such correction and reinforcement it is possible that the form *foots could have been adopted.

Another issue that is bound up with the question of standardization, especially in English, is that of prestige. As standard English is associated with prestigious institutions, and with the education system, it is considered to be a socially desirable variety. There is a widespread assumption that if you want to get on in society then you need to master standard English. But it is important to make a distinction between standard English spelling and grammar, and pronunciation. While it may be important that everyone uses the same spelling and grammatical systems, it is not necessary for everyone to have the same accent. There is, however, a standard accent of English, what is known as Received Pronunciation (RP). This accent is not tied to a particular area of the country like other accents such as Geordie, or Scouse, but rather it is linked with a particular class. Historically RP is the accent of the British Public Schools, the universities of Oxford and Cambridge, the aristocracy and the BBC and consequently it was considered to be socially desirable. Often when people criticize a particular feature of pronunciation, they are comparing it to RP. A good example of this is h-dropping. Because RP pronounces initial /h/ in words like *house* and *hand*, dropping the initial /h/ is seen as an error or a corruption, even though it is in fact an extremely common feature of most English accents. Standards are thus artificial creations, designed to halt language change to enable communication on a particularly wide scale. Where such languages carry prestige, they are often used as a benchmark to measure other less prestigious varieties, leading to the view that these are corruptions of the correct usage.

So far in this chapter we have been considering why languages change and whether it is possible to characterize these as improvements, or corruptions. The point that I have been trying to emphasize is that language change is 'non-teleological': that is, it is not goal-oriented. It is not about progress or decay. We must avoid studying language change with preconceived prejudices and value-judgements. Linguistics is a descriptive rather than a prescriptive discipline and is concerned with documenting and describing changes rather than judging whether they are improvements or corruptions. When newspapers report that a particular change is a corruption or an error, they are being prescriptive in making judgements about usage. As linguists we need to avoid making such judgements and to focus on what people actually say, rather than what they, or others, think they ought to say.

So the study of language change is principally a descriptive activity. But if we stop at simply describing changes then it can quickly become a pretty dismal business. Identifying and describing changes is really just the first stage in the process which should be followed by trying to discover *why* a change happened, and why it happened at that particular time and in that particular way. By assembling a series of such changes and explanations we can then proceed to attempt to explain why languages change and to look for patterns in the kinds of changes that take place and the reasons behind them. There is, however, a difficulty here in that historical linguists have traditionally considered the explanation of linguistic change an impossibility. But more recently historical linguists have drawn upon insights and techniques developed for the study of contemporary language use and sought to apply these to the study of changes that occurred in the past. The development of the discipline of sociolinguistics has led to important insights into the way language varies according to the speaker and the context within which he or she is speaking. To observe variation according to a range of social factors informants are carefully selected according to their gender, age, class, education, occupation and so on. Because a single speaker can vary his or her language according to context, data is also obtained in a range of formats: casual speech, careful speech, reading prose, reading a word list. The result of this is that, where a speaker is found to vary his or her usage, it becomes possible to try to correlate this variation with social or communicative factors and thus to begin to explain how and why speakers vary their language. There are difficulties involved in obtaining data of this kind as people generally speak more carefully when being recorded. This is what is known as the 'observer's paradox': once you start observing people they modify their usage. To avoid this problem linguists have developed a range of cunning tactics, such as getting informants to talk about particularly intense subjects like near death experiences or allowing them to go off on long digressions. Informants are most useful when they are unaware that they are informants, a principle that lay behind one of the earliest studies of this kind of variation. William Labov (1972) studied the inclusion or omission of 'postvocalic' /r/, that is the /r/ that appears after vowels in words like car, hard, jar, in the speech of New Yorkers. To elicit examples of its use in different social contexts he visited three department stores in Manhattan: the upmarket Saks on Fifth Avenue, the middle-class Macy's and the much cheaper Klein's. His method was to go into the store as a customer and ask one of the employees where a particular item was located that was on the fourth floor. When the person replied 'the fourth floor' he would then pretend not to have heard and ask again. The person would then repeat 'fourth floor', more carefully, thus giving him the same data in two different styles. Once on the fourth floor he would then ask a member of staff which floor this was, to compare their usage with that obtained on the ground floor. What he found was that the staff in Saks used /r/ much more than in the lower-class Klein's, while the staff on the top floor, where the luxury goods are kept, used /r/ more than the staff on the ground floor. This study suggests that the inclusion of /r/ is a feature of prestigious usage in New York. Labov also noted that there was often a difference in the use of /r/ between the two different styles of speech, with staff tending to include /r/ more frequently when speaking carefully than when speaking casually. This suggests that the inclusion of /r/ is in fact a linguistic change in progress, which will become more widespread as more people recognize its prestige. This is confirmed by comparing these results with New York speech of the 1930s, such as in the dialogue of black and white films, that show that most New Yorkers did not have /r/ at all, or by comparing it with more recent data that shows that /r/ has become much more widespread.

Another method of obtaining real data that has been used in modern sociolinguistic studies is to become a member of the social group that you wish to study, so that people speak openly and without restraint in your presence. This method also has the advantage that you can study a small group of people in greater detail, allowing you to chart their social situation in a more nuanced way. Labov's division of society into three classes: lower, middle and upper class is rather crude, and in reality people often shift between various social networks. So a person might come from a working-class background but work amongst middle-class people and have married into an upper-class family, meaning that they are constantly shifting between different class groups. The most famous example of this methodology is a study of Belfast speech carried out by James and Lesley Milroy (Milroy, 1992) which showed how speakers with strong ties to their social and geographical origins tended to retain features of the local accent, while speakers who were weakly tied to their origins tended to be innovative in their usage. A common feature of speakers moving between social groups is that they try to adopt features of the accent of the group to which they aspire to belong. A frequent result of this kind of imitation is 'hypercorrection' or 'hyperadaptation': a tendency to overshoot and to produce forms that are not found in the target accent. A good example of this concerns h-droppers attempting to speak RP who frequently add initial /h/ in environments where it does not belong, producing forms like *ham* for *am*.

Clearly many of the issues and methods that we have been considering derive from the study of present-day languages and you might be wondering how relevant they are to the study of past states of languages such as English.

This is an important issue and it is one that I will address in the chapters that follow. But if social and communicative factors are central to the study of linguistic variation and change today, then the same is likely to be true for the study of historical variation and change. Society has of course changed considerably throughout English history, as have the communicative functions for which English is used. But as long as we are careful not to impose anachronistic interpretations upon the evidence, then sociolinguistic insights can help to explain historical variation and change. Perhaps most problematic for the application of this methodology to the study of historical change concerns the nature of the informants: written texts rather than living speakers, and I intend to confront this difficulty in the following chapter.

1.1 Further reading

In this chapter we have considered the distinction between a descriptive and a prescriptive attitude to language change and considered various different ways of approaching the study of changes that have affected the English language during its history. For further reading on the questions of how and why languages change students are recommended to read Aitchison (2001), which draws upon evidence from a number of languages. More advanced discussions concerned with the theories and methodologies practised by historical linguists can be found in McMahon (1994) and Lass (1997). Labov's work on New York speech and other associated studies can be found in a collection of papers in Labov (1972). The Milroys's work on Belfast speech and discussion of social network theory is outlined in Milroy (1992). For a useful introduction to sociolinguistic methods of investigating language variation and change see Hudson (1980).

2   Evidence

In the previous chapter we looked at how modern sociolinguists study linguistic variation and change, involving the collection of data in a range of formats: word lists, connected prose, conversational language and so on. When studying the history of a language all we have is whatever happens to survive. Where modern linguists carefully select their informants according to age, gender, class, occupation and dialect, historians cannot afford to be so choosy. Although modern linguists can obtain all kinds of background information concerning their informants, their place of upbringing, occupation and so on, our informants are generally anonymous scribes about whom we have little or no information. Another major difference is that, where modern linguists are dealing primarily with spoken language, we must work exclusively with written sources. Any analysis of the spoken language must be carefully deduced from study of the written texts. So clearly there are a number of methodological difficulties to be encountered when applying modern techniques to the historical study of language. Bearing all these various caveats in mind, let us begin by looking at the kinds of informants we have: that is, what kind of evidence actually survives for the study of the history of English.

2.1 Old English

Old English is used to describe the language spoken by the various Germanic tribes who migrated to Britain during the fifth century AD. Up to this point Britain was a province of the Roman Empire and so its official language was Latin. This was the language used by the Roman governors and by the British subjects who interacted with them. Prior to the Roman invasion the native language was a Celtic language, although during the Roman occupation

Celtic speakers retreated into the remoter and more peripheral regions of Britain, modern Cornwall and Wales or across the channel to what is now Brittany. Each of these areas remained Celtic speaking for centuries, although Cornish officially died out in the late eighteenth century. The marginal social and geographical position occupied by the Celts during the Anglo-Saxon period means that there is very little evidence of Celtic influence upon OE. The majority of Celtic words that survive in English are in place names (see Chapter 5 for further discussion).

By the middle of the fifth century the Romans had decamped and returned to Rome, leaving a political vacuum. In AD 449, the Celtic king Vortigern responded by inviting Hengist and Horsa to come to Britain and to provide necessary protection against potential invaders. But the Germanic tribes were attracted by the opportunities Britain offered and preferred to conquer and settle. Despite the title 'Anglo-Saxons' there were, according to the historian Bede, three tribes represented by the invaders: Angles, Saxons and Jutes. The invaders initially settled in Kent and parts of the eastern coastline, particularly in East Anglia, and over the following two centuries they spread throughout much of Britain and lowland Scotland. It is not known precisely where these tribes came from, although their homeland was probably the area that is now north-west Germany and southern Scandinavia, as well as the northern part of the Netherlands that is known today as Friesland.

The patterns of settlement contributed directly to the OE dialect map. The Saxons settled in the south of the country, giving rise to place names such as Sussex (i.e. south Saxons), Essex (east Saxons) and Wessex (west Saxons), although the Jutes occupied Kent. The Angles settled in the Midlands and consequently the area north of the Thames stretching to the River Forth in modern Scotland is known as Anglian. The Anglian dialect is divided into two distinct subdialects: the variety south of the Humber is known as Mercian, while Northumbrian refers to the dialect spoken north of the Humber. The southern dialect, known as West Saxon, is divided into two chronological periods: Early West Saxon, the dialect in use in the latter half of the ninth century and associated with the works attributed to King Alfred, king of Wessex from 871–899. Late West Saxon is linked politically with Winchester and particularly associated with manuscripts containing the works of Ælfric and Wulfstan who wrote religious prose works, such as sermons and saints' lives.

This brief description of the dialects of OE gives the false impression that these regions are clearly demarcated and equally well represented, in the same way that a modern dialect like Geordie can be associated with New-castle. In reality the texts that survive in these dialects are few in number and the boundaries that separate the dialects are the subject of considerable scholarly uncertainty. The difficulty of making a truly comparative study of the evidence for these different dialects is compounded by the fact that the surviving texts were copied at different times. The Northumbrian texts are the oldest surviving OE texts, dating from the seventh and eighth centuries, the period of Northumbrian hegemony. These texts include early copies of Cædmon's *Hymn*, Bede's *Death Song*, the inscription on the Franks' Casket and a portion of the *Dream of the Rood* carved in runes on the Ruthwell Cross. In the eighth and ninth centuries the power base was in Mercia and it is during this period that the earliest Mercian texts were copied. These include the Corpus Glossary, the Epinal and Erfurt glossaries and the Vespasian Psalter Gloss. The political dominance of Wessex towards the end of the OE period, the tenth and eleventh centuries, means that the majority of texts written in this period were copied in West Saxon. As the majority of our surviving OE texts were copied during this period, there is considerably more evidence for the West Saxon dialect than for any of the others. Writing in the native tongue, or 'vernacular', received a particular boost in the late ninth century when King Alfred, dismayed by the lack of learning among his people, set in motion a programme of translation of important Latin works into OE. Although it is now thought unlikely that Alfred himself was actually responsible for the translation of all of these works (Godden, 2007), the impetus came from him, as did the decision to have copies made and circulated throughout the kingdom of Wessex. The works Alfred chose for translation were those he considered to be foundational to any education and included a work dealing with the duties of pastoral care, Pope Gregory the Great's *Cura Pastoralis*, a philosophical dialogue, Boethius's *De Consolatione Philosophiae* and Bede's history of the English Church: *Historia Ecclesiastica Gentis Anglorum*. Also associated with Alfred is the beginning of a major work of history, the Anglo-Saxon chronicle, which chronicles national and local events right up to the Conquest, and even beyond in the case of the version that was produced in Peterborough, known as the *Peterborough Chronicle*.

In the tenth century another revival of learning took place, inspired by the Benedictine reform that began with the foundation of monasteries such as Cluny on the continent, spreading to England in the second half of the tenth century, where it was focused on the monastery at Winchester during the period in which Æthelwold was bishop. Ælfric, a prolific vernacular author who, in addition to religious prose tracts also composed a grammar which uses English to teach the Latin language, was a pupil under Æthelwold at Winchester and subsequently monk at Cerne Abbas and abbot of Eynsham.

This brief conspectus of the texts in which the evidence for OE is preserved highlights the difficulty in carrying out a truly comparative analysis. Northumbrian texts of the seventh and eighth centuries are likely to differ considerably from West Saxon texts of the tenth century because of the passage of time as much as because of differences in dialect. As a result it is very difficult to distinguish diatopic differences, differences which are related to geography, from diachronic differences, differences which are related to the passage of time. Another complicating factor is that the language of the various OE texts is likely to differ because of the variety of styles, registers and types of texts that survive. Thus the language of a prose sermon is not strictly comparable to that of a heroic poem and neither is comparable with that of a riddle. To get an overview of the dialect differences found in OE, one would like to compare copies of the same text written in different dialects at the same time. But this kind of evidence simply does not survive. There are, however, some instances of texts written in different dialects which at least allow us to identify important differences between them, even if they are not exactly contemporary. A good example of this is a short poem known as Cædmon's *Hymn*. The story of how Cædmon, an illiterate cowherd, was inspired to compose this poem by an angel is told by Bede in his *Historia*, where he gives a Latin translation of Cædmon's OE poem. The OE version of the poem is first recorded in the margins of two early Northumbrian versions of the original Latin version of Bede's *Historia*, as well as a later version incorporated within the translation of Bede's work into the West Saxon dialect of OE. Placing the three texts side by side reveals some important differences:

West-Saxon version:
Nu sculon herigean heofonrices Weard,
Meotodes meahte ond his modgeÞanc,
weorc Wuldorfæder, swa he wundra gehwæs
ece Drihten, or onstealde
He ærest sceop eorðan bearnum
heofon to hrofe, halig Scyppend.
Þa middangeard monncynnes Weard,
ece Drihten, æfter teode
firum foldan, Frea ælmihtig.

St Petersburg version:
Nu scilun herga hefenricæs Uard,
Metudæs mehti and his modgithanc,
uerc Uuldurfadur, sue he uundra gihuæs,
eci Dryctin, or astelidæ.
He ærist scop aeldu barnum
hefen to hrofæ, halig Sceppend.
Tha middingard moncynnæs Uard,
eci Dryctin æfter tiadæ
firum foldu, Frea allmehtig.

Moore version:

Nu scylun hergan hefaenricaes Uard,
Metudæs maecti end his modgidanc,
uerc Uuldurfadur, sue he uundra gihuaes,
eci Dryctin, or astelidæ.
He aerist scop aelda barnum
heben til hrofe, haleg Scepen.
Tha middungeard moncynnæs Uard,
eci Dryctin, æfter tiadæ
firum foldu, Frea allmectig.

Variant spellings across these three versions of this single, short text provide important evidence for differences in pronunciations, spelling, morphology and lexis. At the level of spelling, the St Petersburg and Moore versions both use <u> to represent the /w/ sound where the West Saxon version uses the letter 'wynn', represented in the edited text by <w>. The early Northumbrian texts also differ from the later West-Saxon version in using <th> rather than the runic letter <Þ> to represent the sounds /ð/ and /θ/. Spelling differences that seem to reflect variant pronunciations include the presence of a diphthong in the West-Saxon *Weard*, where the Northumbrian texts have *Uard*. The diphthong is the result of a major sound change known as 'breaking' which affected vowels followed by certain consonant groups. The spelling of this word in the Northumbrian texts shows us that this sound change did not affect this dialect. The spelling of the word 'heaven' as *heofonrices* in the West-Saxon version also attests a diphthong not recorded in the Northumbrian texts. This is the result of another sound change, known as 'back mutation', which did not affect the Northumbrian dialect. At the level of morphology we can see evidence in the Northumbrian texts for the obscuration of inflexional endings that was a major factor in the transition from Old to Middle English (see further Chapter 6). So, where the West-Saxon text has the inflected form *foldan*, the Northumbrian versions both have *foldu*, showing the loss of the final nasal consonant and the tendency for unstressed vowels to become interchangeable. Finally, at the level of lexis, the Moore version preserves very early evidence for the adoption of an Old Norse loanword. This is the word *til* in line 6, *heben til hrofe*, where the St Petersburg and West-Saxon versions both have the OE form *to*.

Comparative studies of this kind can be very revealing in documenting differences between the OE dialects, although we must always remember that we are not comparing texts that are exactly contemporary but rather texts copied at different times in different locations.

2.2 Early Middle English

The EME period is also sparsely represented in the written record, because of the restricted functions of the vernacular following the Norman Conquest. As we have seen in the previous section, before the Conquest English was the language of Anglo-Saxon chronicles, religious and literary writing. Following the Conquest, Latin replaced English as the language of record and religion, while by the end of the twelfth century French had also become a major literary language. By the middle of the thirteenth century French also took over as the language of the law. During this period English did continue to be used, but it survived largely as a spoken language and was seldom used in the prestigious functions that were written down. Writing in English did continue after the Conquest but many of the earliest instances of early Middle English are in fact copies of OE texts produced in monasteries. These texts frequently provide little evidence for EME as their scribes tended to preserve the features of the OE original very closely so that any changes that may have taken place in their own language are masked.

Very few original English texts were composed during this period. An important exception to this and a seminal text for the study of EME is the *Peterborough Chronicle*. This text is a continuation of the Anglo-Saxon Chronicle instituted by King Alfred which continued to be copied in Peterborough up to 1154, thereby preserving valuable evidence for ME of the twelfth century. The continuations to the *Peterborough Chronicle* fall into two major sections: the first continuation, 1122–1131, and the final continuation, 1132–1154. The first continuation was probably composed by a single monk working on six different occasions, adding material as the events unfolded. The final continuation was probably the work of a different individual, working retrospectively in 1155. The *Peterborough Chronicle* evidence is thus important for a number of reasons: it can be dated, it can be localized (we know it was written in Peterborough) and it covers different periods throughout the early twelfth century (a period in which few spontaneous English texts survive). By the late twelfth century rather more English texts began to appear; some of these are copies of OE texts, but in some of these scribes have updated the language of their exemplars, providing insights into their own language. The thirteenth century saw an increase in the number of English texts that were composed and a number of important texts survive from this period. These include *Ancrene Wisse/Riwle*, a work of spiritual guidance composed for noble women who had taken up life as a religious recluse. The *Ancrene Riwle* was originally addressed to three noble women and survives in seven copies, while *Ancrene Wisse*, a revision of the original work written for a larger group of women, survives in just one manuscript. The text shows similarities with another group of devotional texts addressed to women, such as *Hali Meiðhad*, *Sawles Warde* and a group of female saints' lives. This period also saw the composition of Laȝamon's *Brut*, a verse chronicle written by a Worcestershire priest called Laȝamon, which survives in two manuscripts copied in the second half of the thirteenth century. Another secular literary work of the thirteenth century, surviving in two manuscripts, is the *Owl and the Nightingale*. Despite the greater number of literary texts composed in English in this period, English was rarely used in documentary texts: Henry III's *Proclamation* of 1258 is a rare exception.

This creates a number of problems for the study of Early ME: while the *Peterborough Chronicle* can be dated and localized, most of these texts can only be given approximate dates and rough localizations. A useful way of dating and localizing such texts would be to compare them with documentary texts, such as legal documents, which can be dated and localized, but very few of these survive. One group of texts which can be localized are those copies of OE charters that I mentioned earlier, produced at the big monastic houses like Ely, Winchester and Bury St Edmunds. But the scribes of these charters were extremely conservative and frequently preserved the language of their OE originals very closely, even down to the individual letter forms. By the end of the thirteenth century, scribes of OE charters did begin to modernize the language of their texts, giving us insights into the changes that had taken place in their language in the intervening years. However, this material needs careful interpretation as scribes often retained OE features alongside their own EME.

Dating of EME texts is thus reliant upon internal references, which are few and often very vague, and the dating of the manuscripts in which they survive is generally on the basis of their handwriting. Some EME texts can be connected with particular locales via their author or the provenance of a manuscript. For instance, Orm, author of the *Ormulum*, is thought to have been a canon in the Augustinian House of Sts Peter and Paul in Bourne, Lincolnshire. Laȝamon, about whom we know nothing apart from what he tells us in his *Brut*, states that he was a priest at Areley Kings in Worcestershire. This helps to localize his own dialect, but not necessarily that of either surviving manuscript. The single surviving manuscript of *Ancrene Wisse* was owned by Wigmore Abbey in Herefordshire, and there are various other connections with the south-west Midlands that suggest that it was copied in that area. The linguistic and stylistic similarities between this text and the other saints' lives and devotional works imply that they too were composed in this area. Such associations are useful, but we must always bear in mind the possibility that they do not necessarily tell us anything about the language of the text, which might have been written elsewhere, or might have been written by a scribe trained elsewhere. Another complication is that the copies of the texts that survive were mostly written by anonymous scribes, rather than by the authors themselves, so that we know nothing about the people whose language we are actually studying.

A major problem concerning the linguistic analysis of medieval manuscripts is that we frequently do not know whose language it is that we are studying. Is the language that of the author, or that of the scribe, or some combination of the two? To try to answer this question, we need to take into account the kind of copying practice employed by the scribe who copied the text. When a scribe copied a text he might choose to reproduce his exemplar exactly, as in the case of the copies of Anglo-Saxon charters I mentioned earlier, in which case the language would be that of an earlier scribe, or possibly the author himself. Scribes who copy in this way are known as 'literatim' copyists, that is, ones who copy letter by letter. A well known instance of this kind of copying practice in the EME period is the scribe of the *Owl and the Nightingale* in Cotton Caligula MS A.ix. This text was copied by a single scribe, but it contains two very different linguistic systems, so that lines 1–900 and 961–1174 vary quite predictably from lines 901–60 and 1175–end. The only explanation of this strange situation is that the scribe reproduced exactly an exemplar that was copied by two scribes with different spelling systems. The Caligula scribe was clearly unconcerned by these differences in the text of his exemplar and simply reproduced what he saw in front of him without question. This kind of copying practice is generally thought to have been carried over into the copying of English by scribes trained to copy Latin texts, such as Biblical texts, where the language was fixed and variation was not an option.

However, a scribe might choose not to preserve the language of his original and rather to convert it into his own system, removing all traces of the language of his exemplar. This kind of copying practice, known as 'dialect translation', seems to have been comparatively rare in the EME period, although it was extremely common in the later ME period as we shall see. Another type of scribal behaviour, very common throughout the ME period, is to mix these two policies, producing a *mischsprache*, a language which contains a mixture of scribal and exemplar forms.

An important exception to these generalizations of scribal behaviour are those rare cases of manuscripts copied by the author himself, known as holograph manuscripts. There are two important holograph manuscripts dating from the EME period: Bodleian Library MS Junius 1, containing the *Ormulum* and British Library MS Arundel 57, containing the *Ayenbite of Inwyt*. I have already mentioned that Orm can be connected with a religious house in Bourne, Lincolnshire and the fact that the manuscript is in his own hand suggests that it was written there and that its language represents the language of this dialect *c.* 1200. The fact that the manuscript is not copied from another version means that its language is 'pure', that is, not a mixture of authorial and scribal forms. As well as being in the author's own hand, the *Ormulum* is an important text as Orm devised a regular and consistent spelling system to enable the text to be read aloud. As a result Orm's spelling system provides much useful information about the way the text was intended to be pronounced. To give you an idea of what Orm's spelling system looks like, I have included a brief extract from the *Ormulum* below:

An Romanisshe <u>kaserr-kinğ</u>	emperor
Wass Auğusstuss ȝehatenn,	called
Annd he wass wurrÞenn <u>kasserr-kinğ</u>	
Off all mannkinn onn erÞe,	
Annd he ğann Þennkenn off himmsellf	
Annd off hiss <u>miccle</u> <u>riche</u>.	great; kingdom

The most striking feature of Orm's spelling system is the frequency of double consonants; these were used by Orm as a means of indicating vowel length. We employ a similar practice today, as in the example of *later* with a long vowel sound and *latter* with a short vowel. The difference between PDE usage and that of Orm is that he is much more consistent in applying this principle, so that he uses double consonants to indicate preceding short vowels in *annd* 'and', *off* 'of', *onn* 'on'. The second notable feature is the use of a modified letter *g*, represented here by a *g* with a superscript line above it: *ğ*. Orm introduced this innovation as a means of distinguishing between two sounds that were often confused in OE and EME writing systems. These are the sounds /g/ and /j/, which were both spelled with the letter <ȝ> in OE; the correct pronunciation had to be determined from the environment in which they appeared (see Chapter 4 for more detailed discussion). Orm avoided this problem by using <ȝ> for the /j/ sound and using the letter <ğ> for the /g/ sound (for a facsimile of a leaf of the manuscript of the *Ormulum* see Burnley, 2000). So, as a holograph manuscript written in an idiosyncratic but consistent spelling system, the *Ormulum* is an important source of evidence. Its provenance is also important; Bourne, Lincs, is about fifteen miles north of Peterborough, so that a comparison of the *Ormulum* with the *Peterborough Chronicle* sheds interesting light on how the language of this region changed during the intervening fifty years.

The other holograph manuscript is the *Ayenbite of Inwyt*, signed by its author, Dan Michel, who states that the manuscript was 'ywrite of his oȝene hand'. Even more helpfully Dan Michel tells us that he was a brother of the Benedictine monastery of St Augustine's Canterbury and that he wrote it in the 'Engliss of Kent' in 1340. So not only can we place the language of this text but we can also date it. However, we need to be careful in how we interpret this date of 1340. A surviving record dates Dan Michel's ordination as priest in 1296, which means he was probably born in the late 1260s, making him in his 70s in 1340. Some scholars have interpreted a reference in the preface to his being 'seventy year al round' as intended to be literally true, but seeing as he also describes himself as blind, deaf and dumb I think we can assume that this is not intended to be a true self-portrait. Therefore, the *Ayenbite of Inwyt* was copied in the Kentish dialect in 1340, but its language was probably very conservative for this period and is perhaps more indicative of the Kentish dialect of the late twelfth century. Texts like the *Ormulum* and the *Ayenbite* can help to fill the gap left by the lack of documentary materials for this period: that is, we can use them as 'anchor texts': texts whose provenance is known, by which we may localize other texts which do not contain such information.

Another important source of information concerns those texts that survive in multiple manuscripts. There are far fewer of these in the EME period than there are for late ME. Probably the best instance of this is the *Ancrene Riwle*, where the manuscripts are quite widely dispersed in both place and date. All of the extant copies of the text have also been published by the Early English Text Society, making this a text that can be easily and conveniently compared and collated in this way. Other texts surviving in multiple copies include the *South English Legendary*, a substantial collection of saints' lives, which was composed around 1270–80 in the Worcester/Gloucester area. It survives in twenty-five manuscripts which were copied throughout the country, covering a wide range of dialects and a lengthy time span, with the latest manuscripts dating from the fifteenth century (Görlach, 1974). Comparison of the language of these copies of the same text highlights features that were considered to be either provincial or outdated as the text moved out from its original date and place of production. Of course very few surviving manuscripts are copies of other surviving manuscripts, so that a direct comparison is not possible, but we can make some general inferences about what a particular scribe was copying and so identify likely changes. There is an obvious difficulty here, of course, concerning how we distinguish between changes that are diachronic: that is, changes over time that tell us about the way the language has changed, and changes that are diatopic, geographical changes that tell us about differences between contemporary dialects. Such changes may also be stylistic: that is, a scribe might object to a particular form on stylistic grounds rather than because it was obsolete or dialectal. A good example of this is found in the two surviving manuscripts of Laȝamon's *Brut*. The version of the poem that survives in British Library MS Cotton Caligula A.ix is much more archaic than the version preserved in British Library MS Cotton Otho C.xiii. It used to be assumed that the reason for this was that the Otho manuscript was some fifty years later than Caligula and that the scribe had updated many of Laȝamon's archaic linguistic forms. However, it is now thought that the two manuscripts were copied at the same time, so that the different linguistic choices appear to represent two different stylistic responses to Laȝamon's text.

When thinking about the background and training of the scribes of our EME texts it is important to despatch a common myth that claims that these scribes were Anglo-Normans who spoke little or no English (Clark, 1992). This myth was founded by early editors of EME texts who thought that the spelling systems they encountered in these texts were so confused that they could not be the work of someone for whom English was a first language. The fact that French spelling practices were also being adopted for copying the vernacular contributed to the idea that these scribes were Anglo-Normans with no understanding of the language they were copying. The replacement of English scribes with Anglo-Normans did occur immediately following the conquest, but most of these would have subsequently married and integrated into English society. Monoglot French speaking probably only lasted two or three generations and even then it was mostly the province of the gentry and nobility. By the thirteenth century French was being learned as a foreign language, as is shown by the appearance of grammar books designed for educational use in noble households. Certainly by the thirteenth century the idea of a monolingual Norman copying English manuscripts is absurd. Margaret Laing has written that '[t]he confusion of the monoglot Norman scribe no doubt resides in the anomaly that he finds himself to be still Norman and monoglot in spite of having lived for nearly 200 years in Herefordshire' (Laing, 1999: 259). A more likely explanation for these non-native spellings is that, while these scribes were no doubt English speakers, they were used to copying Anglo-Norman texts as well and probably also those in Latin. These scribes may have been trained in Anglo-Norman copying, and so when they came to copy the vernacular they imposed Anglo-Norman spelling habits upon their English texts. This explanation seems particularly likely when we look at the manuscripts in which these EME texts were copied, many of which contain other works in Anglo-Norman and Latin. For example, Cotton Caligula A.ix, which contains the *Owl and the Nightingale*, also contains two saints' lives and a debate poem in French, as well a prose chronicle in Anglo-Norman. Bodleian Library Digby 86, which preserves unique copies of the ME *Fox and the Wolf* and the only ME fabliau not by Chaucer, *Dame Sirith*, also contains texts in Latin and Anglo-Norman. So it is clear that these scribes did copy texts in all three languages, and it is likely that the boundaries between these languages would have been much less clear-cut than they are in our present-day monolingual English culture.

2.3 Late Middle English

In the fourteenth century the role of the vernacular changed substantially and this had important and far-reaching consequences for the history of the English language.

I have already noted that the thirteenth century witnessed a decline in the fortunes of French, as it ceased to be a native language and became a language that had to be taught to children whose first language was English. An important catalyst for this change was the loss of Normandy to the French crown in 1204, marking a major separation of the two countries. Where noblemen had previously occupied land in both France and England many gave up their French estates in favour of those in England. Anglo-Norman continued to function as a bureaucratic language, but by the late fourteenth century its status was compromised and it was seen as provincial. Its position as a spoken language was also undermined by the frequent portrayal of its pronunciation as provincial. For instance, the chronicler Walter Map spoke scornfully of insular French as 'Marlborough French', while Chaucer's Prioress speaks French 'after the scole of Stratford atte Bowe', in the manner of the London suburbs rather than the royal court. The Hundred Years' War (1337–1453) also contributed towards anti-French feeling and helped to foster an environment in which the English vernacular was favoured over the French language.

Changing social conditions during this period also had an effect on the status of the English language. The latter half of the fourteenth century saw major social changes, following the successive outbreaks of the Black Death which reduced the population by approximately a third. This caused a major labour shortage, leading inevitably to the inflation of labourers' wages and their subsequent rise in the social system. During this period the feudal system began to break up, and the traditional social structure constructed upon the model of the three estates, peasants, clergy and knights, was replaced by a much more fluid system based upon economic ties rather than connections reliant on service and loyalty. A middle class emerged who were literate and wealthy, and who aspired to the literary and social pursuits previously enjoyed only by the nobility. This group consisted of monolingual English speakers, creating a demand for literature in English that was of sufficient status to stand alongside the great literary achievements of the French and Italian vernaculars.

The fourteenth century also witnessed the reintroduction of English in the education system, marked by the decision of the grammar master John of Cornwall to use English in 1349. French continued as the language of the law and parliament throughout much of the ME period, with parliamentary debates being recorded in French until 1386.

As a result of these various social and political changes, the late fourteenth century witnessed a flourishing in the use of English as a literary language, witnessed most famously not only in the work of Geoffrey Chaucer but also in that of his contemporaries: William Langland who wrote *Piers Plowman*, John Gower, who wrote works in English, French and Anglo-Norman: *Confessio Amantis*, *Mirour de l'omme* and *Vox Clamantis* respectively, the *Gawain*-poet who wrote *Sir Gawain and the Green Knight* as well as various other alliterative works.

Not only did this period witness a flourishing of composition in English, there was also a considerable increase in the numbers of copies of these works being produced. Where EME texts often survive in one or two copies, LME works survive in far greater numbers: there are over eighty manuscripts of Chaucer's *Canterbury Tales*, over fifty copies of *Piers Plowman* and Gower's *Confessio Amantis*. Other religious texts were even more popular: there are 113 surviving copies of the instructional poem *The Prick of Conscience*, and over 200 copies of the Wycliffite translation of the Bible. The most widely disseminated secular work of the period, a chronicle known as the *Prose Brut*, survives in over 180 manuscripts.

So the amount of surviving linguistic data is much greater for the LME period than it is for EME. But what about our informants? Are we any better informed about who they were and where and when they were working? As with the EME period we come up against the same problem concerning the anonymity of our scribes and the lack of holograph manuscripts. We know a considerable amount about Geoffrey Chaucer's life: he was born in London in the 1340s and died in 1400. He was the son of a vintner, brought up in a royal household, worked in various departments of royal administration, knew French, Latin and Italian. All of this information helps to inform our analysis of his language, although we still face the problem that none of the surviving manuscripts is in his own hand. Just as with the EME texts, Chaucer's language only comes down to us in copies produced by scribes who were generally anonymous. We saw above that EME scribes tended to copy literatim, preserving the language of their copytext and presumably also that of the author. The evidence of these numerous Chaucer manuscripts will provide insights into Chaucer's own language assuming that LME scribes adopted a similar policy. However, this would not be a safe assumption, as literatim copying was much less common in the LME period than it was in the EME period. Scribes of the later period tended to 'translate' the language of their copytexts into their own preferred system, thereby removing much of the authorial language. As texts were copied and recopied by different scribes with different dialects, so the authorial input became increasingly less apparent. But while this kind of copying means that we have less secure evidence for authorial dialects, it does mean that we have comparatively rich evidence for the dialects of the scribes who copied the texts. In many ways this is more useful, as eighty manuscripts of the *Canterbury Tales*, all accurately preserving Chaucer's language, would provide much less data than eighty manuscripts preserving the various dialects of their different scribes. Because of this scribal tendency to translate into their own dialects we have much richer evidence for dialect variation of the LME period. But a problem still remains: if the language is that of anonymous scribes, then how do we know when and where it was used? This is a considerable problem and one that has been a major stumbling block for historical dialectologists for some time. However, a solution to this problem was proposed by the dialectologists responsible for assembling the landmark publication in this field: *The Linguistic Atlas of Late Mediaeval English* [LALME] (1986).

To overcome the lack of localized LME data the makers of LALME adopted a method of dialect analysis developed for the study of modern dialects. They constructed a questionnaire containing a large number of frequently occurring linguistic items which were particularly prone to variation in the LME period. This questionnaire includes personal pronouns, *she, her, they, them*, determiners, *the, these*, conjunctions and adverbs, *then, after, though*, as well as common nouns and verbs, *be, call, came, church, world* and so on. Having assembled this questionnaire, the editors then applied it to some one thousand LME scribal texts, producing a linguistic profile for each of these. This method is thus similar to that described in the previous chapter where an informant is asked to read a list of words, although of course not all words can be expected to appear in every scribal text analysed. Having compiled linguistic profiles for each of the scribes analysed, the LALME editors then compared these profiles with those of texts where the linguistic provenance was known. As we have already seen, a major difference between the EME and LME period is that in the later period English was used to write legal and official documents. The great advantage of this is that these texts are generally firmly localized and dated by an explicit reference in the text itself. On their own, however, these texts are not terribly useful as they are generally short and formulaic. But when used as 'anchor texts' by which other much longer and linguistically richer texts can be localized, these texts become extremely important. So where we have a short document localized internally to York, we can compare the language of this text with other, longer, texts to determine which are likely to also have been copied in York. The process of localizing a text using this method is known as the 'fit-technique' and using this method the LALME editors were able to localize around a thousand scribal texts whose provenance was previously unknown (Benskin, 1991).

It is important, however, to emphasize the uncertain or provisional nature of such localizations. The localization of a text to York does not necessarily mean that it was written there. It simply means that the dialect in which that text was copied is that of York. If it is the scribe's own dialect, it may mean that he was trained in York, but scribes were mobile and it is quite possible that the text itself could have been written anywhere in the country. If the scribe copied the text literatim, the York dialect may not be that of the scribe but that of his exemplar. In this case the scribe and the place of copying may not be linked to York at all. For the purposes of localization it does not matter whose dialect it is, as long as it is consistent. But for subsequent analysis of the text and its language it is important to bear these caveats in mind.

Given that these scribes were generally anonymous, you may think that the question of whose dialect is being analysed is irrelevant. As it is not possible to carry out any kind of sociolinguistic analysis on these informants, does it really matter whether the language belongs to the scribe or his exemplar? In many cases this is true, although interesting developments in palaeographical studies have resulted in advances in our knowledge of medieval scribes. Palaeography, the study of medieval handwriting, has enabled the identification of individual scribes who copied more than one manuscript, so that we are now able to compare a scribe's output across different scribal texts. The importance of this evidence was recognized by the editors of LALME, who used it to demonstrate the consistent way in which scribes translated into their own dialects. So, for instance, palaeographical analysis of Trinity College Cambridge MS R.3.8 and Bodleian Library MS Rawlinson A.389 showed that both were copied by the same scribe, while linguistic analysis of the two revealed striking similarities even down to minute details of spelling. Such evidence supports the view that LME scribes consistently translated the language of their exemplars into their own dialects. However, more recent work on scribes responsible for copying multiple manuscripts has revealed some interesting differences in their treatment of the language of the texts they copy. Perhaps the best-known example of this is the scribe of the two earliest manuscripts of Chaucer's *Canterbury Tales*: the Hengwrt and Ellesmere manuscripts (Doyle and Parkes, 1978). The language of these two manuscripts is very similar, although there are some differences that suggest changes in the scribe's dialect during the period between their copying (Horobin, 2003). However, the same scribe has also been identified as responsible for copying other literary works, including *Piers Plowman* and *Confessio Amantis*, and there are further differences between his copying of the works of Chaucer, Langland and Gower. But most interestingly for our purposes is the identification of his hand as that responsible for copying an official document: the Petition of the Mercers' Guild of 1386 (Mooney, 2006). This identification is particularly significant because it allows us to compare the scribe's treatment of literary texts with a non-literary document. Comparison of the Mercers' Petition with the scribe's other work reveals considerable differences, suggesting that scribes considered these different types of document as having different linguistic requirements. A summary of these differences can be found in the following table:

Summary of differences in manuscripts copied by the same scribe

Item	Hengwrt	Ellesmere	Petition
SUCH	swich	swich	such
MUCH	muche(l)	muche(l)	moche(l)
IF	yif	yif	if
THROUGH	thurgh	thurgh	thourgh
WHETHER	wheither	wheither	whether

Focusing solely on differences in this way obscures the fact that many features are identical across all three manuscripts, but it does help to show how the Mercers' Petition contains variant forms not found in either Hengwrt or Ellesmere. While these variants are not found in Hengwrt or Ellesmere, they are common in other official documents copied in London in this period. This suggests that the scribe made a distinction between the language he used for literary and non-literary texts, suggesting that, as the vernacular began to be used for a variety of different functions, so scribes experimented with the kind of language that was appropriate for these functions.

As well as identifying new evidence of these scribes at work on other manuscripts, palaeographers have also succeeded in identifying the scribes themselves. Linne Mooney's recent work on the scribe of the Hengwrt and Ellesmere manuscripts discussed above culminated in the identification of his signature in the Common Paper of the Scriveners' Guild in 1392. The identification of this scribe as the professional London scrivener Adam Pinkhurst, presumably the same 'Adam scriveyn' addressed by Chaucer in his short poem, has huge significance for Chaucer studies. But it is also important for our analysis of his language. Not only can we give this scribe a name but we can also sketch out a brief biography: his origins were in Pinkhurst Farm in Surrey and thus he seems to have been an immigrant into London. In addition to copying their petition of 1386 Pinkhurst also kept the Mercers' Account Books, thus providing dated evidence of his copying. These discoveries fill out our understanding of this important scribe, his contexts and connections, thereby shedding light on the factors that may have impacted upon the linguistic choices behind the texts he copied.

As well as manuscripts copied by known professional scribes, the LME period also contains a few rare instances of holograph manuscripts, manuscripts in the author's own hand. Given the huge increase in the amount of vernacular manuscripts produced in the LME period, the number of such holographs is disappointingly small. In fact works of just two authors survive in copies written in their own hands: those of Thomas Hoccleve and John Capgrave. Hoccleve was a Londoner, active in the capital in the generation following Chaucer. As well as composing Chaucerian verse, Hoccleve was a professional scribe who worked in London in the Privy Seal, where he copied documents in both French and Latin. In addition to his day job as a Privy Seal clerk Hoccleve supplemented his income copying literary texts for the London booktrade and parliamentary petitions, just like Adam Pinkhurst (Burrow, 1994). In fact Hoccleve and Pinkhurst must have known each other: both contributed to the same copy of Gower's *Confessio Amantis*: now Trinity College Cambridge MS R.3.2. Hoccleve's works also survive in copies by other professional scribes, allowing us to make comparisons between authorial and scribal copies. As well as shedding light on the way scribes responded to and altered their copytexts, this kind of comparison also reveals errors introduced by Hoccleve himself (Burrow, 1999). The tendency for an author to introduce errors when copying his own works is further witnessed by the two holograph copies that survive of Hoccleve's *Learn to Die*. This is the only one of Hoccleve's works that survives in two holograph copies and so it provides an important insight into the poet's accuracy as well as his consistency in features such as spelling, word division and word order (Bowers, 1989). Here is an extract from the poem in its two holograph copies to allow you to see the kinds of variation tolerated by the author himself:

> To lerne for to die is to haue ay
> Bothe herte and soule redy hens to go
> þᵗ whan deeth cometh for to cacche hir pray
> Man rype be the lyf to twynne fro
> And hir to take and receyue also
> As he þᵗ the comyng of his felawe
> Desroith and ther of is glad & fawe
>
> (Huntington Library MS HM 744, folio 54r)

> To lerne for to die is to han ay
> Bothe herte and soule redy hens to go
> That whan deeth cometh for to cacche hir pray
> Man rype be the lyf to twynne fro

And hir to take and receyue also
As he that the comynge of his felawe
Desroith and is ther of glad & fawe

(Durham University Library MS Cosin
V.iii.9, folio 53v)

While these two extracts are substantially very similar, there are some differences which indicate the type of variation tolerated by Hoccleve. There
are different spellings of the infinitive of the verb *have* in line 1: the Durham manuscript has the contracted form *han* where HM 744 has the full
form *haue*. HM 744 has an abbreviation for 'that', p^t, in lines 3 and 6, where
the Durham MS spells the word out in full, using <th> rather than <þ>.
The Durham MS adds an unnecessary -e at the end of *comynge* in line 6,
where HM 744 spells the word without a final -e: *comyng*. The most substantial difference between the two extracts is the change in the word order of
line 7: HM 744 has *ther of is* where the Durham MS has *is ther of*. None of
these differences has major implications for our interpretation of Hoccleve's
work and only the last has editorial implications; however, they all contribute to our understanding of the nature of linguistic variation in LME. These
variants remind us that even holograph texts could contain variation and
that any attempt to deal only with 'pure' texts that do not contain such variation would be anachronistic.

John Capgrave was an Augustinian friar of Lynn Priory in Norfolk who
wrote theological works in Latin as well as saints' lives in English verse and
prose. Here is an extract from the holograph copy of his life of St Gilbert to
give you an idea of what his dialect looked like:

In þat same seculer lyf and in þat tendyr age, he folowyd, as he coude and
myth, þe reules of religious lyf, and to hem all of whech he had ony power he
ful benyngly gaf exaumple þe same reules to folow. For first he was a maystir
of lernyng to þe smale petites, swech as lerne to rede, spelle and synge. Tho
childyrn þat were vndyr his disciplyne he taute not only her lessones on þe
book, but beside þis, he tawt for to pley in dew tyme, and here playes taute
he þat þei schuld be honest and mery withouten clamour or grete noyse. For
þouȝ he had not at þat tyme experiens of þe good customes whech be vsed
amongis religious men in monasteriis, ȝet had our Lord God at þat age put
in his brest þese holy exercises, for he taute þoo disciples þat he had to kepe
silens in þe cherch; all an on our to go to bedde & eke to her lessones; all
wente þei togidyr to her pley or ony oþir þing.

Capgrave's dialect differs from other varieties in a number of ways. His
spellings *myth* for *might* and *taute* for *taught* show that he no longer pronounced the velar fricative /x/ in these words and so ceased to write them
with the <gh>. Capgrave also regularly has <e> where other dialects have <i>,

as in *swech* 'such', *whech* 'which', and *cherch* 'church', another feature of the East Anglian dialect in this period. His spelling *gaf* 'gave' indicates a pronunciation with initial /g/ rather than /j/, as is found in the work of Chaucer, for example, who writes *yaf*. Initial <h> is found in some words, but not all: it is present in *honest* and *holy*, but not in *our* 'hour'. This may indicate that this sound was unstable in this position in Capgrave's speech, leading to an erratic use of <h> in the written language.

One further category of evidence that emerged towards the end of the LME period is that of the private letter. The best-known example of this kind of evidence is the collection of personal correspondence containing some 360 letters and memoranda written either by or for members of the Paston family, during the period 1425–1503, known today as the Paston letters. This collection of letters is of great importance in preserving spontaneous non-literary usage by a variety of authors. These letters are signed, addressed and dated, so that we know when they were written, who they were written by and to whom they were addressed. This variety of detailed personal information is of course of great significance for analysing the language of the letters themselves. The letters were written by a range of family members, male and female, and covering several generations, enabling us to take account of gender and age when analysing variation within the corpus of letters. We also know a considerable amount about the education and subsequent careers of the members of the Paston family, especially those that rose to social prominence, and we can use this information to understand changes in their linguistic habits. However, not all these letters are autograph, that is, not all were actually written by the person from whom they were sent. About half of the collection, including all the letters from female members of the family, was dictated to professional scribes employed by the family. The period over which the Paston letters were copied is of particular significance for tracing the development of standard English, and these letters are an important corpus of texts for tracing the history of standard written English, as we will see in the next chapter.

2.4 Early Modern English

As with the previous periods in the history of English our primary evidence for EModE is written sources from which we must make deductions about the spelling, pronunciation, grammar and lexicon during this period. But a major technological change separates this period from the preceding one: the advent of printing. The printing press had huge implications for the language, particularly concerning the establishment and dissemination of a standard written language, as we shall see in the following chapter. The mass production of books that came with printing also revolutionized the nature of the book trade. In the period of manuscript production the sale of books was a bespoke trade: a client would approach a bookseller and order a copy of a work which would then be produced for that single client. Printing brought with it speculative production, where large numbers of copies of a work were printed and then circulated to a much wider market. The cost of such books also decreased, allowing books to be owned by a wider cross-section of society. As a result there are considerably more texts surviving from the EModE period, although the new technology meant that there was considerably greater linguistic uniformity in the texts that survive.

The increase in text production during the EModE period led to the emergence of an important new category of linguistic evidence: books written about the language by contemporary speakers. As we will see in the next chapter, the EModE period saw the beginnings of the desire to regulate and standardize the language. One of the consequences of this prescriptive urge was the production of manuals of correct usage. It is in the sixteenth century that we see the publication of the first grammars of English, such as William Bullokar's *Pamphlet for Grammar* (1586), an abbreviated version of a longer work that does not survive. More examples appeared in the seventeenth century, although confusingly some of these are written in Latin rather than English. They include Alexander Gil's *Logonomia Anglica* (1619), Charles Butler's *The English Grammar* (1633) and Ben Jonson's *The English Grammar* (1640). All previous linguistic studies were focused on Latin and it is for this reason that these grammarians used the structure of Latin as the model for the analysis of English. This was unfortunate as it led to the introduction of a number of non-existent grammatical categories into English, as well as the omission of some genuine ones. These grammars do, however, provide us with objective contemporary discussions of the language and so provide a whole new category of linguistic evidence for us to study. Another advantage of these sixteenth-century grammars, especially when compared to their eighteenth-century equivalents, is that they are more descriptive than prescriptive. Because notions of incorrect and correct usage were in their infancy during this period, the discussion of language use is more objective and tends to record actual usage rather than to prescribe some hypothetical usage. Some even include variant usages, showing that they were not totally at the mercy of the desire to regularize and standardize the language; this is obviously useful in giving us access to different varieties of EModE.

There were, however, writers who were concerned with a notion of correct usage, and these provide us with valuable evidence concerning pronunciation and spelling. The orthoepists and spelling reformers were concerned with the correct pronunciation of English and with establishing a spelling system that properly reflected this spoken language. We will consider their proposed reforms in Chapter 4; at this stage I want simply to highlight the usefulness of this kind of material, which provides direct information about the way English was pronounced. But there are problems with this evidence, particularly because there was at this time no standard phonetic notation or metalanguage, that is, technical terminology for describing sounds, and the systems used by particular writers are often highly individual. This means that it is often difficult to be precise about exactly what sound is being referred to. Vowels are described as being 'acute' or 'vivid', presumably meaning close or high, and 'fat', presumably meaning low. Vowel sounds are likened to those used in foreign languages, such as 'Italian a', or to animal noises: 'their sound is not far unlyke the sheepes bae' (Alexander Hume, c.1617), or other noises: like the sound [h] being like the sound you make when warming your hands. Some of these early phoneticians were comparatively sophisticated, although they could be influenced by the spelling rather than by the sound of a particular word. A good exception to this is John Hart, who gives a good account of the phonetic difference between a vowel and a consonant and can distinguish between voiced and voiceless consonants. His description of vowels takes account of length, tongue position and lip-rounding, just as a modern phonetician would, though he does make some errors. Their concern with promoting correct diction meant that the orthoepists were generally prescriptive concerned with condemning provincial and vulgar pronunciations. This prescriptive attitude can lead to a distorted picture of the phonetic situation, although it can also lead to the inclusion of variant and dialectal pronunciations. Another useful publication designed to help users of English was the homophone list: a list of different words with the same pronunciation. For example, Cooper (1687) lists words with 'the same pronunciation, but different signification and manner of writing', for example, bread/bred; hair/hare; coughing/coffin. These lists tell us little more about the actual pronunciation of a word, although their prescriptive ethos means that they include variant pronunciations to condemn them, as found in Cooper's list of vulgar pronunciations, such as *bushop, dud, wull, wuth; shure, shugar; leece* and *meece* for *lice* and *mice*.

Increased literacy in the EModE period led to an increased use of personal letters, providing valuable access to individual linguistic practices. This kind of evidence is particularly important during this period as the standardization of public spelling habits meant that printed books became increasingly fixed in their usages. Private spelling, however, continued to show variation so that letters and diaries are a valuable source of dialect evidence. More widespread literacy meant that women wrote their own letters, providing much greater evidence for gender differences in linguistic habits. The letters of Lady Brilliana Harley to her husband Sir Robert Harley are a good example of this. Her spellings show a mixture of traditional and innovative spellings revealing someone not entirely comfortable with the traditional conventions who was also trying to reflect her own pronunciation in her spelling system. Here is an example from one of her letters.

> I haue sent you vp a litell hamper, in which is the box with the ryte-ings and boouckes you bide me send vp. I pray God presarue you and giue you good sugsess in all your biusnes, and a speady and happy meeting.

The spelling *ryteings* 'writings' testifies to the loss of initial /w/ which occurred in the seventeenth century, while her use of the spelling *rwite* 'write' elsewhere shows the problems that she had reconciling this pronunciation with the conventional spelling. Such evidence enables us to correlate variant pronunciations and spelling practices with specific social and geographical factors. Lady Brilliana Harley was born around 1600 and lived at Brompton Castle near Ludlow in Shropshire and was married to Sir Robert Harley, a prominent politician. Her letters, the majority directed to her son, are mostly written in her own hand over a period from 1638–1643. Just as the Paston Letters enable us to correlate particular linguistic features with specific dates and individuals whose background and careers we are able to trace, so can we make similar inferences from the letters of Lady Brilliana Harley. An important distinction between her letters and those of the Paston family is that here we have a letter in the hand of a female writer, where the Paston women all used amanuenses. So the EModE period differs from the OE and ME period in providing a larger amount of holograph material, especially holograph material written by people whose backgrounds and social networks can be studied. Another important distinction between this period and earlier ones is the increase in non-literary texts, providing access to language used in everyday contexts and thus enabling a more complete picture of the ways in which language was used during this period.

2.5 Further reading

In this chapter we have surveyed the different types of evidence available for the historical study of English. Different periods have their own particular issues, depending on the types of text copied in English and the amount of information that survives concerning their authorship, date and place of production. A problem that is common to all three periods studied in this book is the limitation of our evidence to the written language, so that discussion of pronunciation must always be carried out indirectly. This overview of the three major periods also reveals the way that the amount of available evidence increases between Old and Early Modern English, with the result that the later period appears comparatively rich in texts and contextual information. Perhaps the most crucial difference between the EModE period and the preceding ones concerns the appearance of contemporary discussions of language use, providing us with a window onto linguistic attitudes of the period. However, the prescriptive attitude of these linguistic commentators often complicates the nature of the evidence, as well as encouraging and hastening the drive towards standardization. This desire to standardize and regulate linguistic usage leads to a greater linguistic homogeneity than found in the Middle English period, thereby limiting the value of evidence from this period. The lack of a standard variety in the Middle English period, and the lack of prescriptive attitudes, means that the evidence of dialect variation in this period is much richer than it is for either OE or EModE. So we can see that the process of standardization is an important factor in the history of the language and one that has a huge impact on the type of evidence available and how we examine it. We will look in more detail at this subject in the following chapter. If you want to pursue some of the issues of evidence that have been raised in the current chapter, Smith (1996: 17–24) provides a useful overview of the nature of the evidence available for the historical study of English. There are also chapters on Old and Middle English dialectology in volumes 1 and 2 of the *Cambridge History of the English Language*. Hogg (1988) is an important methodological statement concerning the problems involved in carrying out dialectological study of OE, while the essays in Laing (1989) and LALME (1986) should be consulted for the theory and practice of ME dialectology. The standard work on the EModE orthoepists and spelling reformers is volume 1 of Dobson (1968). For a collection of texts containing samples of everyday English of the EModE period see Cusack (1999).

Standardization   3

In this chapter we will be looking at the establishment of a standard variety of English, a process known as standardization. This raises a fundamental question which we need to address at the outset: what is standard English? There are several key features of a standard language, each of which must be considered in any study of the process of standardization. The most important defining feature of a standard language is its uniformity and resistance to change. Another aspect is that a standard language should be 'supraregional', that is, not tied to any particular locality and can be used by any individual irrespective of his or her geographical origins. Both factors are well-demonstrated by present-day standard English, which consists of a series of rules which enable us to determine whether a word is spelled correctly or incorrectly, whether a sentence is correctly formed or not. Another feature of a standard language is that it is used for a variety of different linguistic functions. Standard English is the language used by our government, legal system and educational system, all of which uses help to reinforce and sustain its continued acceptance as the standard variety of English. Its association with these various institutions also lends it prestige, so that it is the variety that people associate with social advancement. Present-day standard English has also been 'codified': that is, its rules have been set out in various grammar books and dictionaries so that there is a common agreement over what is acceptable and what is not.

While each of these aspects is fulfilled by standard English spelling and grammar, they are less true of the standard English reference accent, known as Received Pronunciation (RP). RP is an accent that is spoken by members of a certain class rather than people from a particular geographical area. In this respect it is clearly a standard or reference accent, although it allows a considerable amount of internal variation, so that John Wells (1982) distinguishes between Uppercrust, or U-RP, mainstream RP, adoptive RP (spoken by people for whom RP is not their native accent) and near-NP, comprising accents that are similar but not identical with RP. Even within these categories there is considerable variation, dependent upon a range of sociolinguistic and phonetic factors.

So, while both written and spoken standards of Present-Day English are considered to be standards, they are different kinds of standard. Jeremy Smith (1996) has introduced a helpful distinction between 'fixed' and 'focused' standards which encapsulates this distinction. Standard written English is a fixed standard in that it consists of a fixed set of rules from which deviation is not permitted. Standard Spoken English, or Received Pronunciation, is a focused Standard, in that it consists of a set of features to which speakers tend. So there is an important distinction here between fixed and focused standards, and it is a distinction that we need to bear in mind when we come to look at the history of standard English. It is also important that we distinguish between standardization in the written language and in the spoken language when charting the history of the process, given that the two processes have occurred at different rates and to different stages of completion.

When thinking about the process of standardization we also need to draw a distinction between social and linguistic aspects of this process. The social aspect concerns what Milroy and Milroy (1985) have termed the 'ideology of standardisation'. This is concerned with the widespread belief in correct usage, and the notion that there are right and wrong ways of using language. The linguistic aspect of standardization is concerned with the process of linguistic change whereby variation is reduced and a greater uniformity is achieved. Clearly both these factors are important in considering the rise of a standard language, and it is frequently difficult to determine whether the ideology of standardization causes greater conformity in linguistic usage, or whether the increased uniformity in usage promotes notions of correct and incorrect linguistic behaviour. It is, however, important that we distinguish carefully between comments about linguistic variation and the emergence of a standard variety when describing the process of standardization. This distinction has too often been blurred in writings on the history of standard varieties. William Caxton commented frequently on the amount of variation found within English and the difficulties it presented him with as a printer (Blake, 1973). But this does not necessarily imply that Caxton took steps to remedy this problem; studies of the spelling systems used in his printed works suggest that he tolerated considerable variation and showed little interest in developing or promoting a standard system (Horobin, 2003). While comments of this kind can be illuminating in testifying to changing attitudes towards linguistic variation, they cannot be used as substitutes for the textual analysis upon which a history of standardization must rely.

It is also important to emphasize that standardization is a linguistic process, and that for a standard variety to be established it must fulfil certain criteria. It is not sufficient for a single variety to appear which shows internal consistency and regularity; this variety must also be adopted more widely and be used for a variety of linguistic functions before it can be termed a standard language. The linguist Einar Haugen has identified a series of criteria for identifying a standard language: selection, codification, elaboration and acceptance (Hudson, 1980). Once a particular variety has been selected as the basis for a standard language it must then proceed to being codified, perhaps through an educational system or an academy, or by the publication of grammars and dictionaries. Following codification this variety must then be elaborated, so that it is employed in a variety of different linguistic registers. A variety that is used only in legal or literary texts is not a standard language; to achieve full standardization it must also be adopted for religious texts, administrative documents and so on. Finally a standard language must be accepted by all users of a language, so that its use is not confined to just public documents but is also found in private documents, such as personal letters or diaries.

3.1 Old English

We will begin our analysis of the standardization of the English language by looking at the emergence of a standard spelling system. In the previous chapter we noted that OE comprised four distinct dialects and that the spelling conventions used in these dialects differed. However, towards the end of the OE period one dialect, Late West Saxon (LWS), became dominant and began to be used outside its native area of Wessex. The prominence of this dialect is due to the influence of the bishop of Winchester, Æthelwold, who, inspired by the Benedictine reform that began with the foundation of monasteries such as Cluny on the continent, put in place a programme of reform of learning and literacy that led to an interest in the vernacular and a flowering of original composition (Gneuss, 1972). One of his star pupils was Ælfric, who became a monk at Cerne Abbas and then abbot of Eynsham and a prolific author of homilies and saints' lives. Ælfric shared Æthelwold's linguistic interests and composed a grammar which uses English to teach the Latin language. Ælfric's linguistic interests are also manifested in the considerable consistency in spelling, grammar and vocabulary found in the manuscript copies of his works. There is even evidence that Ælfric corrected earlier copies of his works to achieve greater consistency and regularity. However, the achievement of a regular and internally consistent variety is not in itself evidence of standardization. A standard language must also be accepted for use by other writers, especially ones outside the native dialect area. In fact LWS appears to have fulfilled this criterion, in that the prominence of the monastery at Winchester led to the adoption of LWS in a number of other ecclesiastical centres, including Canterbury, Worcester and York. LWS was also elaborated, in the sense that it was employed for a variety of linguistic functions: copies of the *Anglo-Saxon Chronicle*, the OE translations of Bede's *Historia* and Gregory's *Dialogues* are all in LWS. Most strikingly, all four of the major surviving OE poetic codices are also copied in LWS, despite the fact that the individual poems were composed much earlier and in different dialects. So was LWS a standard variety of OE? In some ways the answer is clearly yes, though it is important to emphasize that it does not fully achieve standardization. While they do show considerable internal consistency and regularity, manuscripts copied in LWS admit a degree of variation that would be unacceptable in present-day standard written English. This is perhaps clearest in the large poetic anthologies which contain traces of a variety of different dialects deriving from their original composition and processes of transmission. Despite imposing LWS upon these texts, scribes were evidently willing to tolerate a considerable range of non-West Saxon forms. Another limitation concerns its geographical spread. While LWS was clearly elaborated and accepted outside the Wessex area, its influence is mostly associated with ecclesiastical centres, some of which show differences in spelling and vocabulary. There is also evidence that LWS was not accepted as the sole prestigious written variety. Even though there are fewer texts written in the Mercian dialect during this period, this dialect appears to have exerted a rival pressure, reinforced by the monastery at Lichfield. The Mercian literary language flourished in the early ninth century, as witnessed by the Vespasian Psalter Gloss, and continued to hold prestige in the eleventh century when the life of St Chad was written in this dialect. As late as the early thirteenth century, works in English show the continuity of conventions associated with the Mercian dialect. But neither of these two varieties achieved full standardization in that neither was completely fixed, nor were they ever codified.

3.2 Middle English

Having seen the OE period witness the development and establishment of a supraregional standardized variety, it would be easy to assume that the history of standard English is one of straightforward descent from LWS to present-day standard English. But this is far from the case. One of the important effects of the Norman Conquest on the English language was the replacement of the vernacular with French and Latin as the languages of the law, administration, literature and many other prestigious written registers. The result of this was the demise of LWS and with it the loss of the concept of an English standard language. While English did continue to be written down after the conquest, its function was to aid local rather than national communication. As communication on a national level was now to be carried out by Latin or French, there was simply no requirement for a standard variety of English. The result of this was that ME scribes designed and employed local spelling systems: ones that reflected their own spoken language more closely and that could be understood by a local audience. This means that the notion of ME as a single entity is something of an abstraction: the reality is more a series of ME dialects. When studying any other period in the history of English there is generally a single reference variety that is studied, such as LWS or standard English. In ME there was no such variety. A common reference point that is used is the language of Chaucer. This is understandable in that his works, and thus his language, is widely known, but there is no real reason to privilege this language over any other variety. His language is very different from that of the *Gawain*-poet, or William Langland, despite the fact that all three poets were writing at the same time. It is tempting to think that because Chaucer was a 'great' poet, working in London and working for the king, that his language was the standard of the day. This assumption, however, would be quite wrong.

Because of this lack of standard, ME is often characterized as the dialectal phase in the history of English (Strang, 1970). This label is acceptable, as long as we remember that we are really talking about the reflection of dialect usage in the spelling system. Every period in the history of English has dialects; the difference is that in other periods these remain primarily spoken varieties. Think of the situation today. There are numerous different spoken varieties of English, but everyone uses the same written language. If we did not have recording equipment, linguists of the future would have very little idea what accents such as Scouse, Geordie and Brummie sounded like. This is in fact a major problem for the study of historical dialects, apart from in the ME period where the data is much more plentiful. But while ME is correctly seen as a period of considerable dialect variation, scholars have argued for the existence of standardized varieties of English during this period, and we must now proceed to examine the evidence for these.

3.3 Early Middle English

EME was the period in which dialect variation was most fully reflected in spelling, although one variety of EME is often thought to be an exception to this general rule.

This is what has come to be known as 'AB language': so-called because it is represented by two manuscripts, one containing the prose treatise *Ancrene Wisse* (Corpus Christi College Cambridge MS 402) and the other containing various related saints' lives and religious tracts (Bodleian Library MS Bodley 34). Where most EME texts are very idiosyncratic in their spelling habits, these two manuscripts are linguistically very similar. This close linguistic relationship was first spotted by J.R.R. Tolkien (1929), who coined the term AB language in a highly influential essay on the topic. Because these texts are copied by different scribes using a very similar spelling system, Tolkien assumed that this must represent an early attempt to devise and enforce a standard language, presumably within a monastic school or scriptorium. This view was based upon Tolkien's assumption that when a scribe copied a text in a dialect other than his own he would inevitably corrupt it by introducing many of his own forms. The only explanation for the similarity between A and B, according to Tolkien, is that both scribes were trained to write in the same way. Tolkien's view has been very influential in subsequent discussions of these texts and of standardization in ME, although the premise upon which it was constructed has recently come into question. As we saw in the previous chapter, scholars now accept that scribes could in fact copy literatim: preserving the features of the exemplar, whatever dialect it is in. An alternative, and simpler, explanation for the similarity of these two manuscripts has been proposed by Merja Black (1999), who argues that they are literatim copies of an exemplar copied by a single scribe. This possibility is further supported by the fact that the Bodley scribe does not seem to have been completely comfortable using this system and makes a number of mistakes, some of which he later changes into 'correct' AB. This sounds more like a scribe trying to copy a system that was not his own, rather than a scribe trained to write the dialect. This is further suggested by the appearance of certain hypercorrections, which suggest the scribe was aiming to reproduce features of a language that was not part of his own linguistic system. So, for instance, AB retains the OE spelling <hw-> in words like *which, what, when* and so on. At the beginning of the manuscript the Bodley scribe tended to write <w> rather than <hw>, presumably his own preferred spelling for these items. After a while he started to correct these mistakes, adding the missing <h>; from this point he spelled these words with <hw> consistently. But, in his desire to apply the rule that words that begin with <w> in his dialect should begin with <hw> in AB, the scribe started introducing the <h> in words where it does not appear in AB. As a result we find erroneous forms such as *hwenden* for AB *wenden*.

So, one of the primary grounds for the view of AB as a standard language, its use by two separate scribes, appears to be an illusion. The regularity and consistency of the language is indeed striking and this system has clearly been worked out by someone with considerable intelligence. But this does not necessarily mean that it is a standard language; in fact we find many EME scribes doing similar things. The best example of this is Orm, whose system was very deliberately and consistently regular, but this does not make it a standard language. If AB language or Orm's language was a standard language we would expect to find it used in a larger number of texts, especially in ones copied outside the local area. AB language does not seem to have been very influential and only a few other texts copied in the South-West Midlands show traces of its distinctive forms (Smith, 2001). Later copies of the *Ancrene Riwle* do show a number of features of AB language, but this is the result of their close connection with the text of the *Ancrene Wisse*. Perhaps most telling, the oldest of the extant manuscripts, British Library MS Cotton Cleopatra C.VI, which contains annotations and corrections in the hand of the author, is not written in AB but rather in a neighbouring Worcestershire dialect. If AB were really a standard language then surely it would appear in more copies of this and other texts written in the South-West Midlands and in other regions? There are some other South-West Midland texts that show traces of AB features, such as part of the *Owl and Nightingale* in British Library MS Cotton Caligula A.ix, but this is not sufficient to argue for widespread influence of AB language. While AB may be the product of a scriptorium, there is no evidence that it was ever codified, nor that it was elaborated to fulfil other functions beyond the copying of a small group of closely related religious texts, nor does it appear in texts copied beyond its original geographical area in the South-West Midlands. So AB language fails to fulfil any of the criteria set out by Haugen as defining a standard language. Geoffrey Shepherd (1972) seems to have recognized this when he referred to it, somewhat paradoxically, as a local standard: 'The AB language is probably best thought of as a standard but local literary dialect of Middle English.' Rather than seeing AB as a standard language surrounded by various non-standard usages, we should view these as different, but related attempts to reorganize the spelling conventions of the local area to reflect contemporary pronunciations.

3.4 Late Middle English

An important landmark in the identification of the emergence of a standard variety of written English was the publication of an article by M.L. Samuels in 1963. Samuels's study was based upon the examination of large numbers of ME manuscripts as part of the ME dialect survey that resulted in the publication of LALME, described in detail in Chapter 2. As a result of this wide-scale investigation of dialect variation in ME manuscripts, Samuels was able to identify the emergence of groups of manuscripts written by different scribes which appeared to show a greater degree of orthographical uniformity than was found elsewhere. Samuels labelled the language found in these groups of manuscripts Types I–IV. Type I, also known as the Central Midlands Standard, is found in a number of texts associated with, although not exclusively, John Wycliffe and the Lollard movement. This language is found in numerous copies of religious texts and Bible translations produced by the Lollards, copied and circulated widely throughout the country. The language is based on the Central Midlands dialects, particularly counties such as Northamptonshire, Huntingdonshire and Bedfordshire, which were centres of Lollard activity. The mixture of Central Midlands forms that are characteristic of this variety include the following: *sich* 'such', *mych* 'much', *ony* 'any', *silf* 'self', *stide* 'stead', *ȝouun* 'given', *siȝ* 'saw'. Type II is found in a number of manuscripts copied in London in the mid-fourteenth century, such as the Auchinleck manuscript (National Library of Scotland Advocates MS 19.2.1). The Auchinleck manuscript is a large collection of ME romances, many of which are not preserved elsewhere or only in a few later copies. The Auchinleck manuscript was copied by five or six scribes in the London area, probably for the household of a wealthy merchant. Not all of the scribes who contributed to the Auchinleck manuscript were Londoners; two of them used West Midland dialects, suggesting that Type II was not widely seen as a standard variety. Type II differs from earlier London usage in that it shows a marked influence of forms from the East Anglian dialects, a result of large-scale immigration into London from those counties in the mid-fourteenth century. Forms that are characteristic of this variety of London English include the following: *werld* 'world', *þat ilch, ilch* 'that very', *þei(ȝ)* 'though', *þai, hij* 'they'. Type III is the language of the capital in the late fourteenth century, recorded in the earliest Chaucer manuscripts, such as the Hengwrt and Ellesmere manuscripts of the *Canterbury Tales* and the holograph manuscripts containing the poems of Thomas Hoccleve, discussed in Chapter 2, as well as a number of official documents. The mixture of Central Midland and London forms that typify this variety include *world* 'world', *thilke* 'that very', *though, they, yaf* 'gave', *nat* 'not', *swich* 'such', *hir* 'their', *thise* 'these'. Type IV, also labelled 'Chancery Standard' by Samuels, was used by the clerks employed in the various offices of the medieval administration. This language shows the influence of further waves of immigration from the Central Midlands counties, with a number of linguistic features filtered down from the northern dialects. Characteristic features of texts written using Chancery Standard are as follows: *gaf* 'gave', *not, but, such, theyre, thes(e), thorough, shulde*.

An important qualification made by Samuels but ignored by many who have since adopted his findings is that these types do not represent standard languages in the sense that we have defined above. Samuels makes an important distinction between 'standard' and 'standardized' usages, which continue to tolerate a certain amount of variation. This is a similar distinction to that introduced by Smith in his use of the terms fixed and focused standards discussed above: a fixed standard being one which admits no variation (such as present-day standard written English) and a focused standard allowing a degree of variation (such as present-day standard spoken English). The four types distinguished by Samuels are therefore 'standardized', or 'focused', varieties in that they permit internal variation.

Samuels's classification has provided a solid basis upon which future research may build, and new approaches and techniques have helped researchers both to question and refine Samuels's findings. The first problem is this: how widely does a variety need to be accepted for it to be considered a standard? The second problem concerns the amount of variation that such varieties tolerate; to put it in simple terms: at what point can a standardized variety be said to have become a standard? To try to answer these questions we will look at how developments in other fields, especially that of palaeography, have helped to clarify this situation.

Samuels identified Type III usage in a number of texts copied in London towards the end of the fourteenth and beginning of the fifteenth centuries. These texts comprise copies of a number of prominent ME literary works: a copy of William Langland's *Piers Plowman*, Trinity College Cambridge MS B.15.17, two copies of Chaucer's *Canterbury Tales*, the Hengwrt and Ellesmere manuscripts and a single copy of his *Troilus and Criseyde*, Corpus Christi College Cambridge MS 61, as well as the holograph collections containing the poems of Thomas Hoccleve. As well as being used for copying literary manuscripts, Type III also appears in several London documents, including the Petition of the Mercers' Guild, written in 1386. This variety of functions, comprising both literary and administrative uses, lends support to the view of Type III as a variety with elaborated functions. Its appearance in manuscripts containing works by three major vernacular poets, Chaucer, Langland and Hoccleve, also supports this identification. But alongside these examples of Type III usage are a substantial body of deluxe London manuscripts not written in this variety. While the Trinity manuscript of the B-text of *Piers Plowman* is in Type III, there are several other London manuscripts of the B-text of this poem that show no traces of its characteristic features. The earliest and best copies of the C-text of *Piers Plowman* were written in London by scribes preserving Langland's own South-West Midlands dialect (Horobin, 2005). There are other early copies of Chaucer's *Troilus and Criseyde* and *Canterbury Tales* written by professional London scribes using idiosyncratic and dialectal usages that show no attempt to adopt Type III forms. The language of the London poet John Gower continues to show the mixture of Kentish and Suffolk forms that represent the poet's own mixed upbringing, and this is found in numerous copies of his works throughout the fifteenth century (Samuels and Smith, 1981; Smith, 1988). The identification of these and many other instances of London scribes and manuscripts showing no sign of Type III influence highlight the limits of this type as an influential standard. Recent research has also demonstrated how our understanding of Type III needs to be revised even further. In the previous chapter we saw that palaeographical analysis of certain manuscripts and documents written in Type III by Linne Mooney revealed them to be the work of a single scribe. It has long been known that the two manuscripts of the *Canterbury Tales* copied in Type III, the Hengwrt and Ellesmere manuscripts, are the product of the same scribal hand, and other copies of Chaucer and Gower have since been attributed to this same scribe. But more important for our purposes is the recent identification of two of the major witnesses to Type III as copied by the same scribe: the Trinity MS of *Piers Plowman* and the Petition of the Mercers' Guild (Horobin and Mooney, 2004; Mooney, 2006). These findings suggest that the similarities observed by Samuels in the language of these manuscripts and attributed by him to the existence of a standardized variety of London English are in fact due to their being copied by a single scribe. In his identification of Type III, Samuels was particularly impressed by the similarities in spelling habits between the Ellesmere manuscript and the Trinity manuscript of *Piers Plowman*. While he cautioned that 'any form of written standard is conspicuous by its absence', he added that 'perhaps the nearest to it is the type of spelling that is found in both the Ellesmere MS and in Trinity College Cambridge 353 (B.15.17) of the B-text of *Piers Plowman*'. The significance of the similarities between the spellings of these two manuscripts is of course considerably diminished if they are the work of one scribe rather than two. The attribution of the Mercers' Petition to this same scribe serves to undermine the evidence that Type III was elaborated to fulfil a variety of functions, both literary and documentary.

Similar problems of definition relate to Samuels's Type IV, also known as Chancery Standard. I noted above that scholars have often failed to pay attention to the nuanced distinction between standard and standardized usages made by Samuels, and this is particularly true of the work of John Fisher (1996) whose work on the process of standardization presents Chancery Standard as a fixed entity. Fisher, along with Richardson (1980), argues that Chancery Standard was an official standard endorsed and promoted by the king himself as part of a deliberate policy of propaganda. However, there is no evidence for this royal endorsement and promotion. While it is true that Type IV was the variety that formed the basis of our present-day standard variety, the process by which its constituent spellings were disseminated into the provinces was a much more gradual and complex process.

One very important factor in this process was of course the advent of the printing press, set up by William Caxton in the 1470s. The language of Caxton's printed texts was not identical to that of Chancery Standard, but he did broadly follow the same preferences adopted by the Chancery. Caxton was not a linguist concerned with standardizing the language, like Johnson or Swift in the eighteenth century; he was first and foremost a business man keen to exploit the financial possibilities opened up by printing (Blake, 1991). To do this he needed to print books in a spelling system that could be read by the widest possible audience, so evidently he was anxious not to use spellings that would cause difficulties for his readers. But beyond that basic requirement Caxton appears to have had little interest in imposing a regular spelling system on his books. Rather he seems to have carried over many of the spellings associated with the texts he was printing, as seen in the Dutch spellings found in his own translation of a Dutch version of *Reynard the Fox*, for example, *valdore* 'falldoor, that is, trapdoor' and *vlycche* 'flitch'. In translations from French works, like the *History of Troy*, we find a greater preponderance of French spellings, such as the ending -ique rather than -ic in words like *magique, musycque* and *practicque*. That this was not Caxton's preferred practice is shown by the use of *magik, musik* and *practik* elsewhere in his printed works (Blake, 1969). Further evidence of the importance of the exemplar in determining Caxton's spelling practices is found in his editions of the works of poets like Chaucer and Gower, where we find him deliberately retaining dialectal and archaic spelling features associated with those authors (Smith, 1986; Horobin 2003). So John Fisher's (1996: 129) claim that Caxton 'should be thanked for supporting the foundation of a written standard' places too much emphasis on Caxton's role in the process of standardization and needs rethinking in light of the considerable variety in the spelling practices of his editions, and his willingness to adopt variant forms which he found in his exemplars.

Another important aspect of the advent of printing for the process of standardization was that it allowed numerous identical copies to be made of a single work, something that had never been possible in the age of manuscript copying. Where book production was the work of scribes, prone to make mistakes or to introduce their own dialect forms into a text, there was little opportunity for a standard language to spread. Printing meant that texts could be circulated in an identical format and so removed the possibility for variation of this kind. The much greater number of books produced using the new print technology led to a decrease in the cost of books, allowing them to be owned by a wider cross-section of society. All of these factors enabled this new standardized variety to be disseminated widely both socially and geographically.

Another important means by which Chancery spellings were transmitted to the provinces was via lawyers and legal clerks who came to the Inns of Court and the Inns of Chancery for their training, returning to their provincial origins to practise their trade (Benskin, 2004). There was considerable social and geographical mobility during this period, and many young men of middle class and provincial origins went to London to receive their training and then returned home. But it is important to emphasize that the process by which Chancery standard was accepted in the provinces was by no means immediate. Many provincial dialects had their own local prestige and it took some time for Chancery Standard to establish a national prestige which ultimately overcame these local standards. During this interim period 'colourless standards' emerged: these were varieties in which the more unusual and restricted dialect forms had been replaced by forms which were accepted more widely (McIntosh, Samuels and Benskin, 1986). Dialect features that could be easily understood were retained, emphasizing the continued prestige of local usage. It is possible to demonstrate this process by examining the usage of one particular area in this period: that of Norfolk. Norfolk usage is a particularly interesting case as it comprised a number of distinctive forms that are not found anywhere outside Norfolk, such as <x> for /ʃ/ in *shall*, *should* and so on, as well as <qw> for <wh> in *which*, *when* and so on. The following table presents a selection of distinctive regional forms found in regional Norfolk usage of the fifteenth century.

Table 3.1 Regional Norfolk usage

THEM	hem, the(y)m, es
SUCH	sweche, swiche, soche, suche
WHICH	qwilk, qwich(e), wheche, wache
MUCH	mekel, meche, moche, miche
ARE	ben, (h)arn, beth, bien
SHALL	schal, scha, xal
AFTER	efter, aftir, after,
IF	ȝef, yhef, yefe, ȝif, if
PRES.PART	-and(e), -ende, -yng(g)e, -ing

But while Norfolk usage may look odd to us, and probably also to others from outside Norfolk who often made jokes at the locals' expense, it was a prominent and wealthy centre in the fifteenth century. There was a thriving port with connections to the continent and huge amounts of money were made through the export of wool. Members of the wealthy Norfolk middle class and gentry clearly did not feel under pressure to accept the emerging Chancery Standard usage wholesale. Norfolk citizens were secure in their social position and felt no pressure to accommodate their usage to that of the emerging standard. What we see in Norfolk usage of this period is a gradual replacement of the more marked provincialisms with equivalents that were used more widely:

Table 3.2 Colourless Norfolk usage

THEM	hem
SUCH	swiche, sweche
WHICH	wheche, qweche, qwyche, whiche
MUCH	meche, moche, mych
ARE	ben(e), arn
SHALL	schal
IF	if, ȝif
PRES.PART	-yng

In theory, colourless standards could have persisted for some time, but the equilibrium was upset by members of this group who became more socially and geographically mobile. We can see this in the usages of the Paston family, as documented in their collections of letters written throughout the period in which Chancery Standard was influencing local usage. The Paston family was a typically upwardly mobile middle-class family of this period, based in Norfolk, but with a number of ties with London. A number of the male members of the family were educated at Oxford and Cambridge, and several had legal training in the Inns of Court. So the evidence presented by the Paston Letters emphasizes the gradual spread of the standard which affected private spelling habits in the second half of the fifteenth century. Our knowledge of the careers and contacts enjoyed by members of the Paston family enables us to associate changes in their spelling habits with changes in their social and geographical positions. What this shows is that the adoption of Chancery Standard spelling features is closely related to social and geographical mobility. The Pastons who remain in Norfolk are more conservative in their linguistic habits, thereby tending to preserve their local, dialectal spelling system longest. The Pastons who move to London and move into a higher social group, are much more innovative in their linguistic usage, showing the greatest tendency towards the adoption of a standardized spelling system. As a result of their social and geographical mobility, these Pastons are 'weakly tied' to their Norfolk origins and as such they are likely to show evidence of linguistic change as they imitate the linguistic habits of their social superiors. Weakly tied individuals are classic innovators and spreaders of linguistic change, and they are also likely to hypercorrect in their imitation of linguistic features which do not belong to their own native systems. This can be demonstrated by taking a single example from the third generation of Pastons, two brothers known today as John II and John III (Davis, 1983). The example I want to focus on concerns the spelling of /xt/ in words like *right, might, fight*. In a group of letters belonging to an early period in John II's life, the period between 1461–4, John uses characteristic Norfolk spellings such as <gth> or <thg>. But after 1464 John's career changed dramatically; he became a member of the court in the service of the king and was subsequently knighted. During this period of preferment and advancement we also see changes in his spelling system, which shows the replacement of regional features such as <gth> and <thg> with the standard spelling <ght>.

A similar situation is found in the letters written by John III. His early letters, written on behalf of his mother during the period 1460–2, show considerable variation and many dialectal forms; for the *right* group he uses <yth> and <yt>. During 1462–6 John wrote a large number of his own letters, in which the same forms are also found. But in the group of letters in his hand written after 1467 <ght> becomes the dominant form. Just as with his brother, this change in his usage coincides with major changes in John III's career and his social circle. In 1468, he and his brother, John II, accompanied Princess Margaret, sister of Edward IV, for her marriage to the Duke of Burgundy. Later in life he became an MP, was knighted by Henry VIII and was made Deputy Admiral to the Earl of Oxford.

In the case of both Johns it is apparent that their accommodation to the standard language begins when they become socially and geographically mobile. In fact their desire to adopt the correct usage leads them to hypercorrect, producing non-standard, unhistorical forms. If we look again at the evidence of the spelling of the *right* group in the letters by John II and John III we notice that, in their eagerness to imitate the standard by using <ght> rather than any of their own non-standard forms, they hypercorrect and add <ght> in unhistorical positions. So John II uses spellings like *wryght* 'write', and *dowght* 'doubt'. A similar situation is found in the letters written by his brother John III, which include the unhistorical spellings *wright* 'write' and *abowght* 'about'.

3.5 Early Modern English

If the ME period is seen as the age of diversity and variation, the EModE period is often viewed as the period of codification and standardization. There are various factors that helped to contribute to the drive towards standardization that was witnessed in this period so that, before we look in detail at the language itself, it will be useful to sketch out some of these conditioning factors. One of the most significant was the establishment of the printing press. We touched on the specific relevance of this development in the previous section, but here I want to emphasize its broader relevance concerning the promotion of literacy. The increased productivity of the printing press meant that there was much greater access to books, with the result that a wider social and geographical network were able to own books themselves. This period also witnessed improvements in access to education for the middle classes, thereby creating a greater market for such books. Improved social and geographical mobility led to greater interaction between speakers of different dialects, as well as an increased desire to adopt socially prestigious linguistic usages. In the previous section we discussed the emergence and dissemination of a standardized spelling system in the ME period, but by the end of this period there was still no distinction between more and less prestigious forms of speech. Towards the end of the ME period we do see an emergence of dialect consciousness, that is an awareness that people speak differently, but this is not really the same as saying that some people spoke better than others. Perhaps the closest thing to the stigmatization of a different dialect are comments made by John Trevisa in his translation of a Latin chronicle by Ranulph Higden called the *Polychronicon*. Writing in 1387 Trevisa expanded considerably upon the comments made by Higden concerning differences in pronunciation throughout different varieties of English. Where Higden simply notes the difficulties southerners have understanding northerners, Trevisa adds his own criticisms of the northern dialect.

> Al þe longage of þe Norþhumbres, and specialych at ȝork, ys so scharp, slytting [piercing] and frotying [grinding], and unschape, þat we Souþeron men may þat longage unneþe [hardly] undurstonde. Y trowe þat þat ys because þat a buþ nyȝ to strange men and aliens þat spekeþ strangelych, and also bycause þat þe kynges of Engelond woneþ alwey fer fram þat contray: For a buþ more y-turnd to the souþ ...

Here we find a north-south prejudice that is well embedded in English society even today, and it shows the emergence of a tradition that used accent and dialect as ways of marking social difference. So while Higden demonstrates an acknowledgment of dialect variation, Trevisa displays an intolerance and condemnation of the rough and harsh sounds of the speech of northerners. Trevisa was a southerner; he was born in Cornwall but subsequently lived in Oxford and Gloucestershire. His criticisms imply that he regarded the Southern dialects as superior to those of the North, although he also states that the Midlands dialects are the easiest for people to understand, partly due to their central position. But while Trevisa's comments imply that negative attitudes towards different dialects had begun to emerge, it is also apparent that no standard spoken variety of English had yet emerged.

A contemporary example of dialect awareness is found in Chaucer's *Reeve's Tale* (Machan, 2003). This tale concerns two Cambridge students, Aleyn and John, who are northerners. As well as giving the students this northern pedigree Chaucer also gives them northern accents. So their speech includes examples of the characteristic unrounded northern pronunciation of OE /a:/: e.g. *na, banes* where a Southern speaker like Chaucer would pronounce these words with an /o:/ sound: *no, bones*. But these differences are not limited to features of pronunciation. Northern morphology is shown by the use of <-es> endings for the third person singular present indicative in verbs like *behoues* and *werkes*, where we would expect Chaucer's usual forms in <-eth> (for further discussion of these dialect differences see Chapter 6). The students' dialogue also contains a scattering of dialect words. The use of the verb *hope* to express expectation rather than volition in the line 'Our Manciple, I hope wol be deed', was restricted to northern dialects. In the northern dialect this line means 'I think he's going to die', whereas in the South it suggests that 'I hope he's going to die'. But, despite Chaucer's clear awareness of dialect difference in this depiction, this is not a straightforward case of north-south prejudice. Chaucer may have been a southerner, writing for a largely southern audience, but the two students with northern accents are Cambridge undergraduates and of a much higher class than the Miller in the tale who speaks with a southern accent. It is also notable that, despite being tricked by the Miller, they do in fact get their revenge, and it is they that come out with the advantage at the end of the tale.

Another interesting, non-literary, piece of evidence concerning attitudes to dialects in late ME concerns a court case held in York in 1364 (Clark, 1981) During a trial concerning a case of bigamy, the evidence of a witness was dismissed because his pronunciation varied throughout the presentation of his evidence. The witness switched between three different dialects, Scots northern and southern English, and as a result his evidence was deemed unreliable.

An example of a character in a northern dialect text mimicking Southern speech occurs in the Towneley Second Shepherds' Play. In this play a sheep stealer called Mak disguises himself as a royal official and affects a Southern accent to conceal his identity from the other shepherds. The attempt fails and the shepherds see through the disguise, telling him to 'take out tha

Southern tooth, and sit in a turd'. The assumption that a royal official would speak with a Southern accent tells us something of the perception of Southern dialects, and especially that of London, during this period. So, towards the end of the ME period, we see the beginnings of an association of accent with social class. The Southern accent is perceived as being associated with the king and his yeomen, while the northern dialect is seen as being barbaric and unfit for polite conversation. Nevertheless there is no sense of a single standard variety at this time.

In the EModE period this situation started to change so that we begin to see a clear distinction emerge between perceived correct and incorrect ways of speaking (Mugglestone, 1995). This is most apparent in the sixteenth century, when many writers identify a correct form of speech based upon the southern variety, and especially that of London. In 1569, John Hart claimed that the London accent is 'that speech which euery reasonable English man, will the nearest he can, frame his tongue therevnto'. George Puttenham's *Arte of English Poesie* (1589) advises that young poets use 'the vsuall speach of the Court, and that of London and the shires lying about London within lx. myles, and not much aboue'. He also advises against using the language of country people and that of 'a craftes man or carter, or other of the inferiour sort, though he be inhabitant or bred in the best towne and Citie of this Realme'. Alexander Gil made a distinction between country speech and that spoken by gentlemen and women who have 'one universal speech, both in pronunciation and meaning'.

This desire to establish a standard was also driven in part by an anxiety about the status of the language. In the ME period the English language lived in the shadow of its more courtly and prestigious rival French and this was still the case to some extent at the beginning of the EModE period. So the first books printed in England tended to be translations into English of courtly French works, and Caxton frequently lamented the rudeness of his English versions compared to their French originals. But, as English increased its status in the EModE period, it came up against new rivals, particularly in the areas of scholarship and education: the Classical languages. Of course Latin was in widespread use in England throughout the Middle Ages, but it was primarily the language of the Church. In the EmodE period Latin was no longer solely the language of theology but was also the language of science, the language of the works of Copernicus, Galileo and Newton. Latin was not just the focus of much study in this period; it was also the medium of study. This privileging of the Classical languages led to the view that by comparison English was crude and vulgar, unpolished and unable to express complex ideas. English did have its defenders, such as Richard Mulcaster, Head of the Merchant Taylors' School, who argued strongly for the use of English in all areas of study: 'But why not all in English, a tung of it self both depe in conceit, and frank in deliverie?'

While Latin and Greek were favoured over English, the desire to make Classical texts available to a wider readership led to the translation of these texts into the vernacular. Thus the sixteenth century saw numerous translations from Latin and Greek into English, especially by historians, for example Livy and Plutarch, philosophers, for example Plato and Aristotle, and poets, for example Virgil and Ovid. By making prestigious texts of this kind available in the vernacular, these translators imbued English with some of the same status accorded to the Classical languages. The appearance of parallel text editions of Classical texts, with the original text and English translation appearing side by side, also gave English increased status as a language that could stand alongside the Classical original.

Another major factor in the increase in the status of English during this period was the Protestant Reformation. Just as the earlier Wycliffite movement, discussed in the previous chapter, had advocated the translation of the Scriptures into English and had thereby contributed to the advancement in the status of English, so the reformation contributed to the status of English in the EModE period. While Latin remained the major scholarly language of Europe, writers who wished to communicate with a wider audience wrote in English. Many writers used Latin for scholarly works destined for a small and specialized audience, but used English when entering into the heated discussion concerning the reform of the English church. A good example of this is Sir Thomas More, who wrote his scholarly treatise *Utopia* in Latin (1516) but used English when engaging in religious argumentation. The emphasis on the importance of Biblical translation and the importance of access to the Scriptures further contributed to the status of English. One of the earliest of these translators, William Tyndale (1528), explicitly answered these attacks that suggested that the English language was an unsuitable medium for the word of God: 'They will saye it can not be translated in to oure tonge it is so rude. It is not so rude as they are false lyers.' Once English became established as the language of the Bible, following the translation of the Authorised Version in 1611, and was adopted as the language of Church services, its status was much increased. The status of Latin decreased by comparison and following the reformation it began to be seen by some as having Popish or Catholic associations.

One of the major objections to translation into English and its wider circulation was that it was barbarous and rude and not suitable for the treatment of important topics. As a result the earliest writers to use English during this period are defensive and apologetic, but by the end of the sixteenth century they are more confident of the value of works written in English. This change seems to have occurred around 1580 when there is a noticeable change in attitude, following a period of extensive translation into the vernacular, the considerable expansion of the lexicon, the application of the rules of Classical rhetoric to English composition and the achievement of greater standardization. With this change in attitude and a greater confidence and pride in the English language, a sense of nationalism begins to appear among English writers. This kind of nationalistic sentiment differs considerably from that of the Middle Ages, when people saw themselves as members of Christendom rather than of individual nation states with individual identities. Writers consciously sought to produce national epics in the vernacular that could stand alongside the great Classical works of Virgil and Homer, such as Spenser's *Faerie Queene* (1590) and Milton's *Paradise Lost* (1667). Nationalistic sentiments are also manifested in literary works in this period, such as in Shakespeare's play *Henry V*. This nationalistic pride led to a pride in the English language and a desire to see it stand alongside other European vernaculars and even alongside the great Classical languages.

3.6 Further reading

In this chapter we have traced the emergence of standard spoken and written varieties of English. We have seen that standardization is a more complex process than it might appear superficially, involving a series of separate stages: selection, codification, elaboration and acceptance. Applying these criteria helped us to distinguish between 'local standards' which emerged in the early ME period and the national standards that were established in the late ME and EModE periods. Above all this chapter has emphasized the gradual nature of this process, and the way that it was bound up with extralinguistic, social factors, such as the functions of the vernacular, methods of book production, rises in literacy and changing social conditions.

There are a number of more specialized studies that you should consult if you want to pursue this topic in greater detail. For a discussion of the emergence of Late West Saxon and its association with the Winchester school see Gneuss (1972). Smith (2001) provides a useful reconsideration of the existence of a standard language in the EME period, while Black (1999) presents an important response to Tolkien's argument for an AB language. The debate has been summed up in a very readable account by Dance (2003). Samuels (1963) remains the classic account of the emergence of a standard language in the LME period, although it should be supplemented with the important work on Chancery Standard by Benskin (2000) and Sandved (1981). Wright (2000) contains an interesting collection of essays that deal with various theoretical and methodological issues relevant to the development of a standard variety in the period 1300–1800. For discussion of the emergence of a spoken standard in the EModE period see Dobson (1955) and Mugglestone (1995).

4 Spellings and Sounds

4.1 Writing systems

Before we look in detail at the developments that have taken place in English spelling, and its relationship with the spoken language, we will begin by considering briefly how a spelling system operates. Writing systems are often neglected by linguists in favour of the spoken language, but this is unfortunate when dealing with historical periods of the language, given that all our evidence is in written form. While the English writing system is 'phonographic', in that the written symbols map onto sound-segments, the relationship between the spoken and written modes is by no means straightforward. The principle behind a phonographic writing system is that written symbols 'graphemes' represent individual spoken units 'phonemes'. Thus the graphemes <cot> represent the sounds /kot/. If we change the initial sound to /r/, then we change the meaning of the word and thus require a different letter: <r>. It will be apparent from this discussion that angle brackets, <>, are used to indicate graphemes and slash brackets, //, to indicate phonemes. While this might seem fairly straightforward, it is important to be aware that not all spoken distinctions are recorded in the writing system. For instance, there are various ways of pronouncing, or realizing, the phoneme /r/. Northern dialect speakers, particularly in Leeds and Liverpool, commonly use an alveolar tap, [ɾ], while a different realization is found primarily in the North-East, known as the 'Northumbrian burr', consisting of a voiced uvular fricative, [ʁ]. These different realizations are 'allophones' in that they do not change the meaning of the word. You will have noticed that it is usual for allophones to be indicated using square brackets: [ ]. (For more comprehensive discussion of phonetics and phonology and the technical terms introduced here see Jeffries (2006): chapters 1 and 2.) Because they do not have an impact on meaning, allophonic variations are not encoded in a phonographic writing system.

In principle it would be possible to encode such differences, perhaps by using the different symbols employed in the International Phonetic Alphabet, but this would lead to greater complexity for no additional benefit. An important principle of a writing system is that it should be communicatively efficient; that is, it should only encode features that are of communicative significance.

Another important principle concerning writing systems is that the relationship between phoneme and grapheme is conventional; that is, there is no inherent reason why the phoneme /k/ should be represented by the grapheme <k>. This becomes more apparent when we recall that in some English words the phoneme /k/ is represented by the grapheme <c>, while <c> can also be used to represent the phoneme /s/, e.g. *city*. This last example demonstrates that the principle of individual phonemes mapping onto individual graphemes is in fact an ideal, not necessarily followed in practice. The reason for this is that, throughout its history, English has borrowed words from other languages where different conventions are employed. The word *city* is a French loanword and thus employs the French practice of using <c> to represent the sound /s/. So one way in which the principle of individual phonemes mapping onto individual graphemes can be disrupted is by borrowing words from other languages and preserving their original spelling forms. Another cause of disruption is sound change. This is best illustrated by a consideration of PDE spelling, in which a number of words contain graphemes that are not pronounced, such as the <k> and <gh> in the word *knight*. These graphemes were once pronounced but have since ceased to be, so that PDE spelling contains a number of silent letters. So, while we can describe English spelling as a phonographic writing system in which phonemes map onto graphemes, there are a number of exceptions to this basic principle. One of the tasks of this chapter will be to examine the reasons why these exceptions have emerged and the various attempts that have been made to remove them.

The above example of the PDE spelling and pronunciation of the word *knight* raises the question of the relationship between speech and writing. While the spelling system may have been initially designed to reflect speech, it is clearly no longer a faithful record of PDE pronunciation. But this is the result of standardization of the spelling system, a comparatively recent phenomenon, as we saw in the previous chapter. In earlier periods in the history of English the relationship between speech and writing was much closer. In ME texts, for instance, it is common to find numerous different spellings of the same word. But we need to be careful not to assume that all spelling variants are indicative of a variant pronunciation. Spelling variation may have a purely 'graphemic' significance, such as the variation between *shall* and *schall*, where it seems unlikely that the spelling difference reflects a distinction in pronunciation. While different dialects of ME may use different graphemes, or combinations of graphemes, to reflect individual phonemes, they do not necessarily indicate a different pronunciation. A parallel situation exists in the PDE distinction between *colour* and *color*, where one spelling is British English and another American English, although there is no corresponding pronunciation distinction. Where there are differences in spelling that seem to imply a variant pronunciation, we cannot always determine exactly what the different pronunciation is. In the case of ME spellings of the word 'stone', *stan* and *ston*, we can be fairly sure that one pronunciation has an unrounded vowel and the other a rounded vowel. But there are other spelling differences that seem to imply a spoken difference where the phonetic realization is much less clear. For instance, what about forms like *xal* and *sʒal* for 'shall'? These appear to reflect differing pronunciations, but what exactly? The important point to remember is that we are studying primarily the written language, which, in some cases, will reflect some distinction in pronunciation.

4.2 Runes

The earliest writing system used in England is not an alphabetic script at all, but a runic one. Runes were a series of letters designed for inscribing on hard materials such as wood, stone and metals and consequently are comprised of short straight lines. The runic writing system appears to have been first developed in Scandinavia and was brought to England by the Germanic tribes who migrated to Britain during the fifth century AD. This runic system is known as the 'futhark', a name which is made up of the opening six characters, in the same way as the English word 'alphabet' is based upon the opening letters of the Greek system: alpha and beta. But while the runic system adopted for use in England was Scandinavian in origin, a number of developments and modifications took place to give the script a distinctively English appearance. Similar developments are recorded in runic inscriptions found in Frisia (modern Netherlands) and it is unclear whether the Frisian developments were exported to England, or whether the influence went the other way. The adaptations of the older runic system were of two kinds. One kind of development was purely concerned with the appearance of the individual characters and was not connected with the sounds that they represented. A good example of this concerns the *h* rune which in the North Germanic languages is typically represented by Ή, with a single bar. Anglo-Saxon runic inscriptions typically show a development of this form with two bars: Ⴈ. Another development concerns the *k* rune. In the earliest runes this is represented as ᚲ, which subsequently developed to ᚠ; the equivalent Anglo-Saxon rune ᚴ is evidently a further development of this variant.

The second kind of adaptation is the result of changes in pronunciation that separated the Anglo-Saxon language from its Northern Germanic relatives. This is best illustrated by the fate of the ᚠ rune which in Scandinavian represented the sound [a:]. In OE, and in the related language Old Frisian, this sound underwent various changes in pronunciation. Where it was followed by a nasal consonant, [n] or [m], it was pronounced as an [o:] sound. Thus the fourth letter of the Anglo-Saxon runic alphabet represented the [o:] sound, hence the name 'futhork' as distinct from the Scandinavian 'futhark'. In other positions the *a* sound, made with the tongue retracted to the back of the mouth, was fronted, made with the tongue at the front of the mouth. To get an idea of the distinction between these two pronunciations compare the *a* sound in *bath* and *cat*. This change did not affect all *a* sounds, so that the back pronunciation was retained in certain contexts, with the result that two different runes were required for the *a* sound, where Scandinavian had just one. To accommodate these various changes the Anglo-Saxon runemasters carried out certain modifications to the inherited rune. In the Anglo-Saxon futhork the rune ᚠ was used for the fronted vowel [æ], a new rune ᚪ was devised for the low back vowel and the rune ᚩ was employed for the rounded vowel.

Another development triggered by sound changes that affected the Anglo-Saxons concerns the pronunciation of a group of consonants. These are the sounds /k/ and /g/ found in modern English words like *king* and *get*. In OE these sounds developed variant pronunciations depending upon the vowel sound that followed. When they were followed by a back vowel, that is one made at the back of the mouth, they remained unchanged. But when followed by a front vowel they began to be pronounced [tʃ] and [j], like the initial sounds in modern English *church* and *year*. The effects of this sound change can be seen today if we compare modern English words like *church* with their continental Germanic cognates, like German *kirche*. To distinguish between these different pronunciations the Anglo-Saxon runemasters introduced two new runic characters: ᚳ and ᚷ. These new symbols were used to represent the back pronunciations [k] and [g], while the traditional symbols were used for the new front pronunciations [tʃ] and [j].

These changes encapsulate several important themes that will emerge in the remainder of this chapter concerning the ways in which English spelling has developed over the centuries. Some changes are phonetically motivated, that is they are adaptations designed to respond to changes in the pronunciation of the language, while others appear to be little more than changes in fashion: the use of a double-barred h rather than one with a single bar. Such changes may appear of little significance in themselves but contribute something important to the identity of the English spelling system, setting it apart from other related systems used for different languages.

Runic script was employed for a variety of writing tasks, as a simple method of communication, inscribing ownership marks upon everyday objects, writing memorial inscriptions, as well as for recording magical charms. It is the latter aspect of their use that is frequently associated with runes today, though there is little evidence that runes were considered to be primarily associated with pagan religious practices. If that were the case then we would expect the coming of Christianity to signal the end of the runic script but this is not what happened. Instead there was a period in which the runic script and the new Roman alphabet, associated with the new Roman religion, coexisted. Tolerance of runic writing is apparent from a number of significant instances of its use in important Christian contexts. These include runic inscriptions on Christian crosses, such as the famous Ruthwell cross, where a section from the OE poem *The Dream of the Rood* has been added in runes. Perhaps most striking is the runic inscription that was carved on the coffin of St Cuthbert, which was constructed by the monks of Lindisfarne and carried by them from their monastery to its present resting site in Durham Cathedral.

The coexistence of both writing systems is further apparent from the evidence of literacy in both scripts. Evidence of this is found in the survival of runic inscriptions that mix letter forms from both scripts, such as the Chester-le-Street stone inscription of the personal name EADmVnD which uses the m and n runes alongside a number of roman letters. Skilled carvers of runic inscriptions also adopted calligraphic features found in Roman inscriptions, such as the use of serifs at the heads and feet of vertical lines.

4.3 Old English

Following the Christianization of the Anglo-Saxons in AD 597 the Roman alphabet was adopted and the letters used for writing OE are broadly the same as those in use today. As well as being introduced directly from Rome, the Roman alphabet was also imported by Irish missionaries, in the form of the half-uncial script used in Irish monasteries (for an example of this script see the Latin text of the Lindisfarne Gospels of the early eighth century). This cursive script soon developed into a pointed version known as insular script, which was used up to the eleventh century when the continental script known as caroline minuscule began to have an influence. By the end of the twelfth century the insular script had disappeared completely. While the OE alphabet is similar to that in use today, the shapes of the individual letters often differ from our modern equivalents, e.g. <e f g r s>.

As well as differences in the shapes of the individual letters, there are several letters found in OE that are no longer in use, while some letters and combinations of letters (known as digraphs) represent different sounds. This is potentially confusing for beginners who tend to assume that the relationship between letters and sounds found in present-day English is somehow fixed. Studying OE reminds us of the principle introduced above that the relationship between spelling and sound is conventional and that there is no inherent reason why the letter <v> should represent the sound /v/. This becomes more apparent if we compare English with another Germanic language that employs the Roman alphabet, such as German, which uses <w> to represent the sound [v], while the letter <v> represents the sound [f]. One of the problems involved in adopting a writing system developed for a different language, such as Latin, is that the sound system that it represents will not necessarily coincide with that of another language. This was true of OE which had several sounds not found in Latin, such as [w] and the pair of sounds [ð] (as in 'this') and [θ] (as in 'thank'). The solution adopted by the earliest OE scribes was simple: they borrowed the letters used in the runic script to represent these sounds: <þ> 'thorn' and ƿ 'wynn'. As well as using <þ> they also adopted another letter to represent this sound, a variant form of the letter <d>, known as 'eth': <ð>. These two letters were used to represent both [ð] and [θ] indiscriminately and no attempt was made to use one letter for each sound. As well as these additional letters, OE scribes also used a modified form of the letters <a> and <e>, known as 'ash' after the rune that reflected the same sound, used for the sound [æ]. OE scribes also employed a variant form of the letter <g>, adopted from Irish use, known as insular g and written <ᵹ>. It is usual in modern editions of OE for editors to replace ƿ 'wynn' and insular g with their modern equivalents, that is <w> and <g>. In OE the letter <g> was employed to represent two different sounds: the voiced velar stop [g] and the palatal approximant [j], the sound represented today by the letter <y>. While distinguishing between the two uses can be difficult for students, the palatal sound is generally found before front vowels as in the words gēar 'year' and geard 'yard', while the velar sound is found before back vowels, e.g. gōd 'good' and gold. It is customary for modern editors of OE texts to add a dot above the <g> when it represents the sound [j]. A similar rule governs the pronunciation of the letter <c> which has the velar sound [k] before back vowels, as in cuman 'come', but represents the palatal sound [tʃ] when it appears before a front vowel, as in cild 'child'. The letter <k> was only used very occasionally at the beginnings of words to represent [k] when it was followed by a front vowel, e.g. kyning 'king' rather than the more common spelling with initial <c>: cyning. Editors often dot the <c> when it represents the palatal sound as a guide to students.

Another method of representing sounds not present in Latin was to combine two letters to form a digraph. This was the solution adopted by OE scribes for the representation of the sound [ʃ] which was spelled <sc>. As the sound [sk] was not found at the beginnings of words in OE there was no possibility of confusion over its pronunciation. There were instances, however, of its use at the ends of words where confusion is possible, as in *tusc* 'tusk'. Another unfamiliar combination of letters used in OE is <cg> which represents the sound [dʒ] in words like *ecg* 'edge'. In an attempt to rule out any possible confusion some scribes added a silent <e> after <sc> and <cg> to act as a diacritic indicating that the consonants should be pronounced as palatals, e.g. *sceolde* 'should', *hycgean* 'think', although these spellings were not widespread.

OE did not use the letters <v> and <z>, used in present-day English to represent the voiced fricative sounds [v] and [z]. These sounds did appear in OE but their use was conditioned by their position in the word. Where <f> appears initially and finally it is always pronounced [f] and where it appears medially it was pronounced [v]; compare *wulf* and *wulfas*, PDE *wolf*, *wolves*. The same is true of the voiced and voiceless fricative pair [s] and [z], so that initially and finally <s> is pronounced [s], e.g. *hūs* and medially it is [z], e.g. *hūsian* (compare the PDE contrast between the noun *house* and the verb *house*). Because of this system there was no need for different letters: the pronunciation was predictable from the placement of the letters in a particular word.

Another key difference between the OE and present-day English spelling systems is that in OE there were very few silent letters; in most cases all the letters were intended to be pronounced. Speakers of present-day English are so accustomed to the presence of silent letters that they often fail to recognize that such spellings are relicts of previous pronunciations. So, for instance, the word *knot* is spelled with an initial <k> because in OE it was pronounced that way, as is shown by the OE spelling *cnotta*. This same principle also applies to silent letters at the ends of words, such as the now-silent <b> in *lamb* or *comb* (OE *lamb*, *camb*). In fact OE has many instances of consonant clusters that look very unusual to speakers of present-day English, such as *fnæst* 'breath', *gnorn* 'sorrow', *hlēor* 'cheek', *hnæpp* 'cup'. In all such cases each of the consonants should be pronounced. We noted with the example of *cnotta* that in some cases these consonant clusters have been retained despite a change in pronunciation, while in others it is apparent that the simplification of the pronunciation has led to a similar change in the spelling. In many cases the initial consonant of the group has simply been lost as in words like *hring* 'ring'. In words beginning with <hw-> in OE the initial [h] has been lost, but the traditional spelling continues to be reflected in the present-day spelling <wh>. Thus OE *hwæt* is now pronounced with initial [w] but spelled *what*. In Scots the initial aspirate has been retained and so the spelling with <wh> reflects the pronunciation more closely than it does in southern varieties of English.

4.4 Middle English

The English consonant system has remained relatively stable throughout its history and the system of consonants found in ME does not differ much from that of OE. The most obvious differences concern the loss of the runic letters thorn and wynn and the modified letters <ð> and <æ>. These were replaced by their modern equivalents <th>, <w>, <a>. The changes happened at different rates and thorn continued to be used right up to the end of the fifteenth century when it was finally dropped. By contrast <ð> became obsolete by the end of the thirteenth century along with <p>.

As well as these straightforward replacements, the ME period also saw the tidying up and resolving of certain ambiguities in the OE spelling system. For instance, OE scripts used an insular form of g <ᵹ>, which could be used to represent three sounds: the velar fricative [x], the velar stop [g] and the palatal [j]. OE scribes who used insular g for both [g] and [j] encountered a problem in distinguishing between [g] and [j] in initial position. To avoid this confusion some scribes used <i> for [j], while others adopted the practice of using <e> as a diacritic to indicate the palatal nature of the preceding consonant: thus PDE *yoke* could be spelled either *ioc* or *ʒeoc*. The Norman Conquest saw the replacement of the insular script with a Carolingian variety, and it is from this script that our modern form of closed *g* is derived. This Caroline *g* was used mainly for [g], but could also be used for [dʒ]. This form was known in Anglo-Saxon England, but was used mainly for the copying of Latin texts. The insular *g* form continued to be used in the ME period and is known as yogh <ʒ>. In ME <ʒ> was used extensively for the voiceless palatal and velar fricatives [ç x] as well as for [j]: hence its name yogh.

During the ME period, the influence of French practice led to the use of <y, i> for /j/, while <gh> was adopted as a replacement for /x/. This led to the establishment of our modern system where initial [g] is <g>, [j] is <y> and where <gh> is used for [x] (although this is no longer pronounced).

There were also changes in the spelling of the palatal consonants. Where in OE <c> was used to represent /k/ before back vowels and /tʃ/ before front vowels, this was tidied up to avoid any potential ambiguities. So <k> was used for /k/, especially before front vowels where there was potential for confusion between /k/ and /tʃ/, e.g. *keen*, while <c> remained in use before back vowels, e.g. *can*, *could*, and the French spelling <ch> was adopted for / tʃ/. <c> before a front vowel was used to represent the sound /s/, following French practice, e.g. *citee* (Fr cité). The OE <sc> for /ʃ/ was replaced in ME by <s(c)h>. The palatal consonant [dʒ] was initially spelled <gg> or <g>. Use of <g> initially to represent [dʒ] (as in *gesture*) meant that there was potential for confusion with [g] which could appear for some front vowels. This was remedied by the use

of <u> as a diacritic to indicate when the <g> represented the velar consonant, thus the distinction between *guest* and *geste* 'feat'.

French spelling practices were also adopted to represent vowel sounds,
such as the use of <u> for the high front vowel [y] (as in modern French
tu), which had previously been spelled <y> in OE. This sound was however
unrounded in all dialects of ME, except the west Midlands, and was other-
wise found only in French loans, making the use of the French convention
seem more explicable. This also had the advantage of freeing up the letter
<y> to be used in other ways, such as, as an alternative to the letter <i> in
words where a number of adjacent minims, single strokes of the pen of the
same height, used to form the letters <i, n, m>, could cause confusion. The
use of <u> for /y/ meant that another letter was needed to represent /ʊ/ and
/u:/, and these were drawn from French practices. So <o> was adopted for
/ʊ/, especially when surrounded by minims where there was potential for
confusion, e.g. *come, son*, while <ou, ow> were used to represent /u:/, e.g.
hour, house. In the consonant system ME inherited the French practice of
using <qu> for /kw/, cf. modern French *quoi*. So where OE had used <cw> in
cwēn, ME has *queen*.

French also had an impact on the English sound system which had a further knock-on effect upon the writing system. This influence concerns the
English fricative system, that is the consonants that are made by allowing a
small quantity of air to pass between the teeth and lips: [v, f, ð, θ, s, z, ʃ, ʒ].
These fricative consonants can be grouped in pairs depending upon the way
they are produced, or what is called the place of articulation. So [f] is a labio-
dental fricative because it is made by placing the top teeth onto the bottom
lip. [v] is also labio-dental but it differs from [f] in that it has voicing, that is it
is produced with vibration of the vocal folds. So the only difference between
[f] and [v] is the presence or absence of voicing. The same is true of the other
pairs of fricatives, that is [s] and [z], [ð] and [θ], [ʃ] and [ʒ].

As we saw in the previous section, OE had both voiced and voiceless
fricative sounds but each pair was represented by a single grapheme, so that
both [f] and [v] were spelled <f> and both [s] and [z] were spelled <s>. The
way that you can tell whether it is the voiced or voiceless sound is by its
position in the word: where <f> or <s> appears intervocalically, that is
between vowels, it is voiced, elsewhere it is voiceless, thus the word *finge*
begins with [f], while the <f> in *ofer* is pronounced [v], *sunu* has initial [s]
and *wisian* has medial [z]. This system works fine as long as the two sounds
are always kept apart in this way and as long as there are no instances where
the choice of either the voiced or voiceless fricative can affect the meaning of
the word. In OE these sounds were in 'complementary distribution'; that is
it was the position in the word that indicated the correct pronunciation. The
distinction between these voiced and voiceless fricatives was 'allophonic' and

there was consequently no need for a written distinction. It may seem strange to us today not to have separate graphemes to represent this distinction, but a writing system that employed different letters to distinguish allophones would be unduly cumbersome. If we consider our present-day writing system then we see that there are allophonic distinctions that are not distinguished by different graphemes. For instance, the word *laurel* contains two different realizations of /l/. The first <l> is a 'light' l, pronounced [l], while the second is a 'dark' l, pronounced [ɫ]. The choice between these two realizations is governed by their placement in the word and does not affect the meaning of any word. Consequently there is just one way of writing /l/ irrespective of its pronunciation. In principle it would be possible to encode allophonic distinctions in the writing system, but this would be unnecessary and communicatively inefficient. As we saw in the introduction to this chapter, a key principle of writing systems is that they are economical, in that they aim to encode only distinctions that are meaningful.

But the OE system was disrupted by contact with French which does have a phonemic contrast between voiced and voiceless fricatives. During the ME period words of French origin were borrowed into English so that minimal pairs were created such as *fine* and *vine* or *seal* and *zeel*, where the presence or absence of voicing alters the meaning of the word. In such a situation it is not possible to use one grapheme to represent the two sounds without causing considerable confusion. As a result the new letters <v> and <z> were introduced.

The fortunes of the labio-dental fricatives /θ/ and /ð/ are rather different, due to the infrequency of the voiced fricative /ð/. The phoneme /ð/ has a comparatively marginal status in English, it tends to appear in function words and there are few minimal pairs (cf. *thigh* and *thy*, *loath* and *loathe*). The voicing of [θ] in these words appears to have occurred later than [s] and [z], although there is evidence that it had occurred by the late fourteenth century; Chaucer rhymes *sothe*: *to the*, showing the voiced sound. Because of its marginal status no attempt was made to introduce a graphemic distinction between /ð/ and /θ/. This is particularly marked when we recall that ME had three different ways to represent these sounds, that is <þ, ð, th>, but at no point do scribes consistently employ different graphemes for the voiced and voiceless fricatives.

Another important set of ME changes affecting the OE fricative system concern the OE phoneme /x/, similar to the sound in Scots *loch*, or German *nacht*, which appeared in all positions: [h] in initial position, [x] medially and before consonants, and finally as [x] after back vowels and as [ç] after front vowels. Loss of [h] began in the eleventh century in initial consonant clusters, e.g. <hn hl hr>, so that we see ME *lauerd* (OE *hláford*), *nesche* (OE *hnesc* 'soft'), *ringe* (OE *hring*). The next stage in the development was the loss of [h] before [w] which affected dialects differently and is particularly common in the south. In Northern ME and Scots dialects it is written <quh>, reflecting a different pronunciation; present-day Scots still pronounces this group of words with /ʍ/, cf. the minimal pair *witch* and *which*.

The loss of prevocalic [h], that is the [h] sound before vowels in words like *hand*, *have*, is also a ME phenomenon, even though it is often thought to have occurred in the eighteenth century. The reason for this discrepancy is that it is easy to equate the beginning of a sound change with the point at which it becomes noticed or stigmatized. While it is true to say that the eighteenth century is the time when h-dropping became remarked upon and socially stigmatized, there is considerable evidence that [h] was already unstable and prone to loss in many dialects of ME. Of course here we are dealing with spelling evidence so it is difficult to be certain that spellings without initial <h> reflect pronunciations without initial [h], but this does appear to be a reasonable deduction.

The omission of <h> is first attested in texts from as early as the eleventh century, although it is East Anglian texts of the fifteenth century that show the most consistent examples, including both spellings showing loss of <h> and ones showing the addition of unetymological <h>, e.g. *herthe* 'earth'; *hoke* 'oak', *herand* 'errand', *howlde* 'old'. The history of this process of [h] loss in native words is made more complicated by the fact that French loanwords that came into English during the ME period did not pronounce initial [h] because of the loss of [h] in late Latin, which affected all the Romance languages (compare Latin *homo* 'man' with French *homme*, Spanish *hombre*, Italian *uomo*) These French loanwords are regularly h-less in ME, *erbe*, *ost*, although they were subsequently re-spelled with <h> by analogy with Latin, cf. *herba* and *hostem*. So, even though the initial [h] was not pronounced, words like *honour*, *heir* were increasingly spelled with initial <h> in ME, although throughout the ME period much variation is found, e.g. *heir*, *eyr*, *here*, *ayre*. The pronunciation of [h] in present-day RP is probably the result of a restoration of [h] during the eighteenth century, a period of intense prescriptivism. However, even with this prescriptive movement to support its reinstatement, [h] was never restored in some French loans, such as *honour*, *heir*, while in *hotel* and *historian* it was very recent, as shown in *an hotel* and *an historian*.

The ME period also saw the loss of the final voiceless velar fricative /x/, which was accompanied by a shift in some positions of [x] to [f] (e.g. *rough<ruh*). It is hard to date these changes very reliably because the written evidence is complicated by the fact that the <gh> remains even when the sound has either changed or been lost, as is witnessed by PDE *rough* and *night*. We do however find some instances of spellings with <f>, particularly in texts produced in the west Midlands, e.g. *thurf* 'through' (OE *þurh*), *dafter* 'daughter' (OE *dohtor*). In some cases both forms are found, as witnessed by PDE *dough* and *plum-duff*. The loss of this sound occurs earliest before /t/, as is shown by spellings like *douter* 'daughter' and *broute* 'brought', and by rhymes such as *'bright*: *night*: *white'*.

4.5 Early Modern English

The spelling of EModE is much more familiar to PDE readers than that of OE or ME. It shows considerably more consistency and the relationship between spelling and sounds is closer to that of our contemporary spelling system. It might therefore seem as if there is little to discuss in this section dealing with the relationship between spelling and sound in the EModE period. But in fact this is a period in which the spelling system and its effectiveness as a means of representing the spoken system came under widespread scrutiny, leading to a wealth of publications on the subject. The issue was taken up by a group of spelling reformers, concerned with changing the spelling system to create a closer relationship between speech and writing. Another group of reformers had a quite different goal: they wished to see the spelling system changed to reflect the etymology of the words, thus widening the gap between spelling and pronunciation. The increase in literacy in this period led to a concern with the teaching of English to children and thus to a debate concerning the best way of educating children in a system that is rife with inconsistency and complexities. The result was a series of publications concerned with explaining the rules that lie behind the spelling system and the means by which they may be learned. Inevitably such concerns also led to a desire to see the spelling system fixed, so that children can be taught the accepted way of spelling a word, rather than simply one of several variant spellings. As a result, such works often make a contribution to the ongoing debate concerning the standardization of the language and its spelling system.

The desire to establish a fixed spelling system was clearly related to the ideology of standardization associated with the emergence of a standard accent that we discussed in Chapter 3. But it was also driven by a wish to see English as a worthy rival to the classical languages. By comparison with their fixed spelling systems English spelling appeared chaotic and unstable and so greater stability and fixity was seen as necessary to ensuring its enhanced status. The desire to establish a single fixed spelling system was also associated with teachers, such as the Suffolk schoolmaster Simon Daines, whose *Orthoepia Anglicana* (1640) aimed to set down rules for correct spelling and pronunciation as a guide to pupils learning the language. The reform of English spelling was treated by a number of books on spelling which were published between 1540 and 1640, each proposing various reforms of the spelling system, some more radical than others. The major concern of these spelling reformers was the lack of correlation between spellings and sounds. This was in part a problem inherited from the ME period when Norman French conventions were applied to the spelling of English words. But it was further complicated in the EModE period as spelling became standardized and pronunciation changed, leaving the gap between spelling and speech even wider. As part of an attempt to accord greater status to English, the spellings of certain English words were altered to align them with their presumed Latin etymons, the words from which they were thought to derive, creating a further discrepancy between spelling and sound. So the letter <b> was added to the ME spellings *dette* 'debt' and *doute* 'doubt' to align them with the spelling of the corresponding Latin words (*debitum* and *dubitare*), even though they were borrowed directly from the French. The letter <c> was added to ME *vitailes* to give *victuals* (Latin *victualia*); <u> was added to ME *langage* to give *language* (Latin *lingua*); a <p> in ME *receite* (Latin *receptum*); <l> in ME *samon* to give *salmon* (Latin *salmo*). In some cases these changes led to a corresponding change in pronunciation. For instance, ME *aventure* became spelled *adventure* because of the Latin form *adventura* and so the pronunciation was changed, as was ME *avis*, which became *advice* by comparison with Latin *advisum*. But in many cases these changes simply widened the gap between spelling and pronunciation.

The view that spelling should reflect both pronunciation and etymology was satirized by Shakespeare in his play *Love's Labour's Lost*, which draws upon many of the debates concerning the nature of the vernacular in this period. His character Holofernes is a pedant who insists on correct usage and who favours etymological spellings, arguing that etymologically respelled words should be pronounced as they are written. This leads him to propose that the unhistorical <b> in words such *doubt* and *debt* should be pronounced, along with the <l> in *calf* and *half*, as he explains in the following speech:

He draweth out the thred of his verbositie, finer then the staple of his argument. I abhore such phanatticall phantasims, such insociable and poynt deuise companions, such rackers of ortagriphie, as to speake dout *sine* b, when he should say doubt; det, when he shold pronounce debt; d e b t, not d e t: he clepeth a Calfe, Caufe: halfe, haufe: neighbour *vocatur* nebour; neigh abreuiated ne: this is abhominable, which he would call abbominable, it insinuateth me of *insanire: ne intelligis domine*, to make frantique lunatique?

(Love's Labour's Lost, 5.1.17–23)

Holofernes's desire that spelling should reflect pronunciation leads him to propose changes to pronunciation rather than changes to the orthography. A more common solution proposed by reformers at the time was to reform spelling to reflect pronunciation, although in some cases analogy with other English words led to further complications in the relationship between writing and speech. The words *light* and *night* were once pronounced with a medial fricative consonant, hence their spelling with medial <gh>. But in the ME period this fricative sound was lost in such words, though because of standardization the spelling remained unchanged. This meant that *light* and *night* were now pronounced identically with *delight*, which was never pronounced with a medial fricative sound and which in ME is spelled *delite*. But to tidy up the inconsistency of having two words with the same pronunciation spelled differently, the word *delite* began to be spelled *delight*. Superficially this might seem like a logical step, though of course it would have been easier to simply remove the <gh> from *light* and *night* thereby bringing their spelling closer to their pronunciation.

It was a desire to restore the link between spelling and sound that motivated the spelling reformers of the sixteenth century. One of the earliest of these reformers was Sir John Cheke, the Regius Professor of Greek at Cambridge University, whose interest in spelling stemmed from his involvement in the Cambridge controversy over the correct pronunciation of Classical Greek which raged throughout the 1530s. This controversy was sparked by Erasmus, who proposed that the pronunciation of classical Greek should be based upon a reconstruction of its sound system using the written language, rather than on the contemporary pronunciation of Greek. This debate led to a reconsideration of the nature of the English spelling system and its adequacy as a means of representing the English sound system. As well as producing works on spelling reform, Cheke produced a complete translation of the Gospel of St Matthew in a reformed spelling system of his own devising. In his desire to tidy up the problems presented by final <e>, Cheke used doubled vowels to indicate length, e.g. *taak, haat, maad, mijn* and omitted final <-e> in words where it had no function, e.g. *giv, belev.* Where both <y> and <i> were used for [ɪ]. Cheke used only <i>, e.g. *mighti, dai.* Cheke's reforms were systematic but idiosyncratic, representing little more than his own preferences. The following is an extract from his translation of the Gospel of St Matthew:

Jesus heering yᵢˢ went from ýens in a boot himself aloon into á wildernes. yᵉ pepil heering yᵢˢ cām and folowed him out of yᵉ citees on foot. Jesus cōming forth and seing great resort eer piteed ýem and healed ýeer diseased. And whan it was som thing laat, his discipils cam vnto him and said, This is á wild place, and yᵉ tijm is wel goon, let ýis resort go

now, ỹᵗ ỹᵉⁱ maí go into villages and ỹemselves sōm meat. ỹei have no
need said Christ to ỹem to go awaí. Giue yow ỹem sōm meat.

(Sir John Cheke, From the Gospel of St. Matthew)

Another Cambridge scholar who supported Erasmus's reformed pronunciation of classical Greek, Sir Thomas Smith, published the first tract advo-
cating reform of the English spelling system: *De recta et emendata linguæ
anglicæ scriptione dialogus* (1568). Smith argued that the number of letters
in the English spelling system should be the same as the number of 'voyces
or breathes in speaking and no more, and neuer to abuse one for another'.
Where sounds exist in English for which the roman alphabet does not provide an equivalent letter, a new letter should be introduced rather than 'abus-
ing' existing letters by making them represent more than one sound. Smith
thus proposed introducing a number of new letters into the alphabet, some
of his own devising, while others were introduced from Greek and from earlier varieties of English. So Smith proposed that the letter <g> should only be
used for the velar /g/ sound, while the sound /dʒ/ should be represented by
the reintroduction of the OE insular *g*: <ᵹ>. Smith appeals to OE usage in his
proposal to use <c> for /tʃ/, reserving the letter <k> for the sound /k/. For the
sound /ð/ Smith employed two different letters, the Greek delta <Δ> and what
he calls 'thorn d', that is the Anglo-Saxon letter 'eth': <ð>. For the sound /θ/
Smith proposed a further two letters, one Greek and the other derived from
OE: the Greek theta <θ> and the OE thorn <þ>, giving spellings like θ*in* 'thin'
and þ*ik* 'thick' and Δ*öu* 'thou' and ð*ër* 'there'.

In 1569, John Hart, a Chester Herald, published his Orthographie, subsequently elaborated as *A Method or Comfortable Beginning for All Unlearned
Whereby They May Bee Taught to Read English* (1570). He also wrote a third
work, *The opening of the unreasonable writing of our inglish toung*, although
this was not published in Hart's lifetime and survives only in a manuscript
dated to 1551. In this work Hart begins by listing the sounds of English
what he calls 'voices', and he claims that a writing system should contain
the same number of letters as there are voices in the language. The problem with English is that there are not as many letters as sounds and so the
writing system is 'corrupt'. Hart claims that English suffers from what he
calls 'superfluity' in that many words contain superfluous letters (i.e. letters which are not pronounced), such as the <b> in *doubt*, the <gh> in *eight*
the <h> in *authority* and so on. Hart believed that a spelling system should
reflect pronunciation not etymology and that silent letters were an unnecessary feature of English spelling. Their only useful function was to indicate
where a preceding vowel is long, as in *hope*, though he proposed using
accents for this purpose. A further problem was what he called 'usurpation'
the use of a letter to represent more than one sound, as in the <g> of *gentl*

and *game*. So Hart's view of spelling is that each phoneme should map onto a single grapheme, and that no grapheme should represent more than one phoneme. In many ways this is a sensible, if slightly over idealized, situation, and in fact some of the reforms introduced by Hart have been adopted. For instance, before Hart the letter <j> was not a separate letter but was used as an alternative for <i>, often at the ends of words or in roman numerals. Hart advocated using it as a separate consonant to represent the sound /dʒ/, as we still do today. The same is true of <u> and <v> which were used interchangeably, with <v> appearing at the beginning of words and <u> in the middle of words, irrespective of whether they represented the vowel or the consonant. Hart's innovation was to make <u> the vowel and <v> the consonant, so that their use was dependent upon the sound rather than their position in the word. The use of <j> for /dʒ/ meant that <g> no longer had this value and so could be used unambiguously for /g/, while he also reorganized the use of <c> and <k> so that <k> was always used for /k/, leaving <c> for /tʃ/, thereby returning to an OE spelling practice. All silent letters were abolished in Hart's system, as were digraphs such as <ch>, <sh>, <th>, which he represented using specially constructed characters. But these innovations were too radical to be adopted.

In his *Book at Large, for the Amendment of Orthographie for English Speech* (1581) William Bullokar avoided inventing new characters, which he considered the reason for the failure of his predecessors, although he did introduce accents and other diacritics which proved just as off-putting to the general public. He added little new to the theory or practice of spelling reform, although his zeal as a committed teacher to promote an improved system for the benefit of his pupils led to the publication of many pamphlets and translations promoting his revisions.

Perhaps the most effective and influential of the spelling reformers of the sixteenth century was Richard Mulcaster, whose *Elementarie* (1582) presented a more balanced solution to the problem of English spelling. Mulcaster was headmaster of the Merchant Taylors' School and later of St Paul's School in London and his *Elementarie* was designed to function as a textbook to be used in schools. Mulcaster attempted to negotiate a compromise between the ideals of his predecessors and the actual system in place. He understood that no writing system could ever be truly phonetic and that the use of a single letter to represent two sounds was perfectly acceptable. He also recognized the inevitability of the discrepancy between spelling and sound, given that pronunciation was constantly changing. Mulcaster's proposals were based upon sound, reason and custom; his concern was more with explaining and rationalizing the current system than attempting to impose new innovations of his own design. Mulcaster did note some of the confusions in the English spelling system that others attempted to remove, such as the 'weak' and 'strong' pronunciations of <g> which 'semeth to giue som matter to confusion in our writing'. But Mulcaster was less interested in reforming the spelling system to remove such inconsistencies and to promote phonetically consistent spellings and more concerned with the promotion of a single spelling for each word. At the end of his book he gives a General Table of the spelling of the 7000 commonest words, many of which, though not all, are identical to those used in present-day English. The list includes many high-frequency grammatical words that are in their PDE spelling, *through, such, after, again, against*. But there are differences from PDE usage; for example, the use of <ie> rather than <y> in words like *anie, verie*, and of <k> instead of <ck> in words like *quik, stik, pik*. One further feature of EModE spelling variation that is perpetuated by Mulcaster concerns the use of <u> and <v>. While he explains that <v> is always used to represent the consonant and <u> the vowel, he does not observe this in practice and treats the two as positional variants. So we find in his list spellings like *auenge* 'avenge' and *vpon* 'upon'. Despite the objective and descriptive attitude shown by Mulcaster in this work, his list of spellings does include some of his own innovations. For instance, Mulcaster objected to the inclusion of a <u> after 'strong' <g> in words like *guest* and *guess* and advocated its omission. In the list of words at the end of the work these words are spelled *gest* and *gess*, reflecting Mulcaster's prejudice rather than current practice. Mulcaster also felt that <ph> for /f/ in Greek loanwords could easily be replaced by <f>, making such words easier to pronounce by speakers illiterate in Greek or Latin. He lists such words under <ph> in his list, but adds a marginal note questioning the necessity for such spellings: 'Why not all these with f?' In fact the word *pheasant* appears under both <f>, *feasant*, and <ph>, *pheasant*.

In addition to Mulcaster's list of common words the spelling system employed by the early printers provided a model for private spelling habits. The practical difficulties encountered by compositors responsible for setting the type and thus for the spelling system used led to a tolerance of variation in spelling. This was partly driven by the need to justify the ends of lines of texts for which variable spelling was a distinct advantage. So where orthoepists and spelling reformers considered spelling from a theoretical standpoint, for the printers and compositors it was a more pragmatic concern. To make matters more complicated, many of these compositors were recruited from the continent and did not speak English fluently. This led to the introduction of some of their own spelling conventions, such as the Dutch convention of using <gh> for /g/ in words like *ghost* and *ghest* 'guest'; or the use of <oe> in *goed* 'good' which appear from time to time in some of Caxton's editions, though only 'ghost' has been adopted into the standard language. Another practical consideration which might influence the spelling of individual words was the availability of type. The most extreme example of this concerns the letter <þ> which was frequently replaced with <y>. This practice originated in the Northern dialects of ME where the letter <y> was used for both <y> and <þ> (Benskin, 1982). While early printing type did include a thorn, it was frequently replaced by <y> in printed texts. It became particularly associated with the definite article *ye* and in abbreviations, such as *yt* 'that', with the result that the definite article *ye* has survived in mock archaic shop names like Ye Olde Tea Shoppe. The influence compositors and printers had over the spelling systems employed in the works they printed is apparent from Mulcaster's *Elementarie*. As we have seen, this work ended with a list of recommended spelling forms for numerous common English words. It is striking, however, that not all of these recommended forms appear in the printed text which accompanies them. For example, the word *through* is spelled as the PDE form in Mulcaster's list but in the text both *through* and *thorough* appear. Similarly the spelling of *though* recommended by Mulcaster in his list is the PDE spelling, whereas this spelling is never used in the text; here we see the spelling *tho*, without the <gh>. While Mulcaster prefers to use a single <k> at the ends of words, as we have seen, there are instances of the <ck> spelling in the text itself, e.g. *musick*.

By the end of the sixteenth century a common core of acceptable forms had been established and in most cases these were the basis of the present-day standard spelling system. Once this core of spellings had been established and the battle for spelling reform appeared to be lost, the reformers redirected their efforts at the design of transitional alphabets. These were intended to function as a compromise between reformed and traditional alphabets and to enable pupils to master the complexities of English spelling in a more gradual and accessible way. Once again the school teachers led the way, as demonstrated by Edmund Coote's *The English Schoole-maister* of 1596. This work is not intended to offer a reformed orthography, but rather presents a more phonemic system as a bridge to acquiring the traditional system. The most successful of this variety of scripts is that formulated by another school-master, Richard Hodges, in his *The English Primrose* of 1644. This transitional system employed special accents, known as 'diacritics', to indicate the length and quality of vowels and a system of underlining to indicate letters that are not to be pronounced. The second half of the seventeenth century witnessed the publication of tracts aimed at promoting an international alphabet and which attempted to devise letters to reflect the sounds found in all languages. This aim was particularly associated with prominent scientists of the period, such as John Wallis's *Grammatica Linguæ Anglicanæ* (1653) and John Wilkins's *Essay towards a Real Character and a Philosophical Language* (1668).

In the eighteenth century the focus was on fixing English spelling rather than on reforming it. The great linguistic authority Dr Johnson was dismissive of attempts to reform spelling and their lack of success, arguing that no spelling system should be adapted to 'imitate those changes, which will again be changed, while imitation is employed in observing them' (Preface to *The Dictionary*). Rather than changing the language, writers like Swift and Addison wished to fix it to prevent further corruption. This desire to standardize the language inevitably focused on the spelling system, as this is the aspect of the language that is most easily regulated. A further objection to spelling reform arose from changing attitudes to pronunciation. One of the principles of spelling reform had been to bring the spelling system in line with current pronunciation. Eighteenth-century attitudes to pronunciation, however, were highly prescriptive and there was no sense that spelling should be reformed to accommodate the corrupt and ignorant pronunciation that was common.

Despite this desire to standardize the spelling system, private spelling habits continued to tolerate considerable variation so that eighteenth-century diaries and personal letters show a variety of different non-standard spellings. While most writers adopted the conventions of the standard in their public writings, they continued to use their own private spelling systems in personal documents. This is perhaps most striking in the case of Samuel Johnson, whose *Dictionary of the English Language* of 1755 is often viewed as one of the defining moments in the standardization of the language. Certainly a dictionary does provide an authoritative reference work upon which private spellings might be modelled. But Johnson saw his role as recording current usage rather than promoting correct spellings. As he writes in the Preface to the *Dictionary*: 'I have often been obliged to sacrifice uniformity to custom; thus I write, in compliance with a numberless majority, *convey* and *inveigh*, *deceit* and *receipt*, *fancy* and *phantom*.' Johnson's acceptance of current spelling habits in the *Dictionary* is further apparent from his tolerance of variant spellings in the headwords. For instance, the headword *complete* may be found under both spellings *complete* and *compleet*. There are other inconsistencies in his *Dictionary* that he made no attempt to clear up, such as the use of single or double consonants in final position, as in *downhil*, *uphill*, *distil*, *instill* and the use of <ou> or <o> in words like *anteriour* and *exterior*. This suggests that, while Johnson recognized the national standard for his public writings like the *Dictionary*, he was also tolerant of variation. This is also apparent from spelling systems he used for his private writings, where we find *complete/compleet, pamphlet/pamflet, stiched/dutchess* and *dos/do's/does* (Osselton, 1963, 1984)

The tolerance of spelling variation in private writings was quite common in the seventeenth and eighteenth centuries. Writers like Addison and Dryden, for instance, used a large number of variant spelling forms in their private writings, such as letters and diaries. These private spellings do not appear in their printed works which follow the accepted standard spelling conventions. So, by the end of the eighteenth century the English spelling system had achieved almost complete standardization, at least in public documents issued by the printing presses. Some variant spellings remained, such as *honour/honor* and *centre/center*, and it is only in the early nineteenth century, in the work of Noah Webster, that these variants become selected as distinguishing British and American usage. Webster set out as a spelling reformer but subsequently modified his stance to focus on the promotion of a standard American usage that would have a separate national identity from that of British usage, as well as removing some of the unnecessary complexities and inconsistencies of British spelling. Webster published a series of books designed to be used by American school children, including a hugely influential *Elementary Spelling Book*, known popularly as the 'Blue-backed speller'. Here Webster promoted various American spellings that still survive today, such as the use of -er rather than -re, e.g. *theater, meter*, -or rather than -our, e.g. *honor, favor*, and of single consonants before suffixes beginning with vowels e.g. *traveled*. The widespread success of the speller helped to ensure the success of these reforms, as did the subsequent authority of Webster's 1828 *An American Dictionary of the English Language*, which also adopted the reformed spellings. This dictionary was a revised and updated version of Webster's 1806 *Compendious Dictionary of English Language* which contained a number of more radical reformed spellings, such as the omission of final -e in *fugitiv, definit*, the replacement of <ou> with <oo> in *soop*, and of <ea> with <e> in words like *fether*.

4.6 Further reading

This chapter has provided an overview of changes in the spelling of English from the runic writing of OE to the spelling reforms of the EModE period. What we have seen is that such changes have been driven by two principal, often contradictory, impulses. The first of these represents the belief that English spelling should closely reflect pronunciation which has led to the introduction of spelling reforms designed to achieve a closer correspondence between spelling and sound. The second impulse stems from a belief that the spelling of a word should reflect its etymology rather than its pronunciation, and as a consequence spelling reforms have been implemented to reflect Classical spelling rather than contemporary pronunciation. The spelling system that has emerged therefore presents a considerable mixture of conventions, reflecting the spelling conventions of the languages with which English has come into contact, and the differing interventions made by spelling reformers.

If you want to pursue this subject further, then it is worth reading the overview of English spelling from OE to PDE presented in Scragg (1974), although his treatment of the ME period has been made considerably out of date following the publication of *LALME* in 1986. For more up-to-date discussion of ME spelling practices and their relationship to spoken systems see the essays collected in Laing (1989) and an important discussion by Stanley (1988). Sampson (1985) provides a useful theoretical introduction to writing systems, while Smith (2007) contains some important insights relevant to the historical study of English.

The Lexicon 5

5.1 Word formation

Before we begin our discussion of the processes by which new words are formed in English, it will be helpful to begin by considering the nature and the structure of an English word. Superficially, the category of word may appear to be a relatively straightforward linguistic concept to grasp. Words are clearly marked in the PDE writing system in that we leave blank spaces between them, although if we look at older English texts then we find that the boundaries between individual words were less clear-cut. We have seen in Chapter 3 that the spelling of individual words was much freer in earlier varieties of English and as a consequence it is not always apparent whether two forms are variants of the same word or two different words. This problem also applies in PDE in the case of variant forms created by adding endings onto words, like the plural ending -s, or the past tense inflexion -ed; do these endings create new words or just different forms of the same words?

To answer this question we must introduce a linguistic category that is less familiar but which enables us to break down the concept of a word into smaller units. This category is known as the morpheme: the smallest unit of grammatical analysis. A word may be made up of a single morpheme, or it may consist of combinations of morphemes. For example, the word *mean* consists of a single morpheme, while *meanness*, also a single word, is made up of two morphemes: *mean* and *-ness*. The same is true of words like *meaning* and *means*, while the single word *meanings* is made up of three morphemes. But while all of these are morphemes, they differ in the way that they can be used. That is the morpheme *mean* can appear on its own, while *-ness*, *-ing*, *-s* and so on can only be added to other morphemes. This difference gives rise to another important categorical distinction between 'free' and 'bound' morphemes: free morphemes are ones that can appear alone, while bound morphemes must always appear in combination (see Jeffries, 2006: 3.2, 3.3)

This discussion of free and bound morphemes helps us to develop a more sophisticated understanding of what a word is. It comprises a free morpheme, known as a 'stem', combined with a number of optional bound morphemes, known as 'affixes'. Affixes consist of prefixes, which appear at the head of the stem, such as un-, dis-, re-, and suffixes, which appear at the end of the stem and include -ness, -ment, -ful. To complete this definition we must introduce a further distinction: between affixes that create new words and those that create variants of the same word. Those morphemes that create new formations, such as prefixes and suffixes, are known as derivational morphemes, while those that form variants of the same word are known as inflexions. So, returning to the above examples, the addition of the derivational suffix -ness to the adjective *mean* forms the new noun *meanness*, whereas adding the inflexional morpheme -s to the verb *mean* produces the third person singular present tense form of the same verb. It is also important to note that there is a major difference between prefixes and suffixes: suffixes can create new word classes whereas prefixes cannot. So if we add the prefix un- to an adjective like *open* we form another adjective: *unopen*. If we add the prefix un- to the verb *wind* we form another verb: *unwind*. But if we add the suffix -ness to the adjective *open* then we form a new noun: *openness*.

In addition to adding prefixes and suffixes to existing words, there are two further methods of word formation: compounding and conversion. Compounding describes the process by which two or more words, or free morphemes, are used to create a single new word. Examples of this process in PDE are words like *blackbird* or *lunchbox* which are composed of two independent words, i.e. *black + bird* and *lunch + box*. This may seem a relatively straightforward concept, but the identification of compounds is not always so clear-cut. In the cases of *blackbird* and *lunchbox* the fact that the words are joined together makes clear their status as single words, but is this always a reliable guide? What about *train station, swimming pool* or *waiting-room*? Are these compounds or separate words? What these examples show is that we must not rely on spelling, word division or hyphenation to identify compounds. While the spelling of the word *blackbird* alerts us to the possibility that it is a compound, this is of no help in the spoken language. In speech we rely on patterns of stress: there is a difference between *black bird*, with stress on the word *bird*, and *blackbird*, where the stress falls on the initial syllable *black*. Compounds also differ in the way they form their plural. So the plural of the compound *bookcase* is *bookcases*, not *books cases*, which is what it would be if it were two separate words. Another feature of compounds is that they comprise a 'head', in the case of blackbird the word *bird* and a modifier, the word *black*. This is important as it enables new combinations to be formed and to be understood by speakers who have not previously encountered them. But while a *blackbird* is a type of bird and a *lunchbox* a type of box, not all compounds can be analysed so straightforwardly. For instance, a *turncoat* is a compound made up of the words *turn* + *coat*, but it is not a type of coat. This exemplifies a special type of compound known by the Sanskrit term 'bahuvrihi', also known as an 'exocentric' compound, where the true head of the compound is external to the compound itself. In the case of the example 'turncoat' the true head is a person (one who turns their back on their principles), rather than the internal head *coat*.

The final type of word formation that we must consider is 'conversion', so called because it results in the conversion of a word from one grammatical category to another. It is also known as 'zero-derivation', because it forms new words without adding anything to the existing word. Examples include the formation of the verb *bottle*, meaning to put something in a bottle, from the noun without any change to the word itself. A recent example of this process, showing its widespread use today, is the proliferation of the verb *google*, meaning to look up something using the Google search engine. Verbs formed this way can be inflected like any other verb, so that we can easily form constructions such as 'I googled it' and 'Have you tried googling it?' Any word class can be formed by conversion, apart from function words like pronouns, prepositions and conjunctions, although function words can be subjected to conversion, so that the preposition *near* can be used to form the verb *near*.

All languages rely on processes of word formation for the addition of new words to the lexicon, although the importance of this procedure in relation to other methods, especially borrowing from other languages, can change over time. In the first section of this chapter we will examine the importance of word formation in the history of English, paying particular attention to its changing status in the shift from Old to Middle English.

5.2 Old English

Word formation was a particularly important means of adding to the word-stock during the OE period and as a consequence OE had a considerable range of affixes. In addition to the large number of such affixes, many OE affixes had a much wider range of meaning than their PDE equivalents. The prefix un- provides a good example of this as it survives into PDE where its use is primarily to indicate negativity, e.g. *unhappy*, or, when added to verbs, it has a reversative function, e.g. *unlock*. Both of these uses are common in OE, as in the adjective *unbrād*, literally 'unbroad', i.e. 'narrow', and in the verb *unbindan*, un + bind, i.e. 'loosen'. But in OE the un- prefix could also have a pejorative sense, as in the word *undǣd*, literally un + deed, meaning 'wicked deed', or *unweder*, which meant 'bad weather'. Another example is the prefix in-, which generally had the same meaning as it does in PDE, as seen in words like *ingān* 'go inside'. But it could also have an intensifying function, as in the adjective *infrōd*, in + *frōd* 'wise', meaning 'very wise'.

OE also had a rich set of suffixes, many of which were derived from independent words. For instance, *dōm* is an independent word in OE meaning 'judgement', but it was also used as a suffix to derive abstract nouns with the sense 'state' or 'condition'. So it was added to the adjective *wīs* 'wise' to create the abstract noun *wīsdōm* 'wisdom', the condition of being wise, and added to nouns like *martyr* to create the word *martyrdōm* 'the condition of being a martyr'. The large number of suffixes available in OE is apparent from the number of alternative methods of forming nouns with the sense 'state, rank or condition', and which therefore overlapped with the uses of -dōm. These include the suffixes *hād*, which could also function as an independent word meaning 'state' or 'condition', e.g. *cildhād* 'childhood', -scipe, e.g. *frēondscipe* 'friendship', -rǣden, e.g. *hierdrǣden* 'guardianship', -lac, e.g. *brydlac* 'marriage', -nes, e.g. *clǣnnes* 'cleanness, purity'.

By the tenth century this rich system of affixes had begun to decay and as a consequence the range of meanings associated with the prefixes was reduced. This is particularly apparent from the way that OE writers began to use prefixed and unprefixed forms interchangeably. To demonstrate this shift in the importance of key prefixes let us examine the range of meanings associated with the OE prefix ge-. When added to a verb this prefix indicated perfectivity and result: when added to the verb *ascian* 'ask' it formed the verb *geascian* 'learn by asking', when added to *rǣden* 'advise' it formed *gerǣden* 'bring about by advice'. When added to nouns it indicated collectivity, so that *gegeng* means 'fellow travellers' and *gebroþor* 'brethren', or associativity, as in the case of *gefara* 'one who travels with another'. When combined with an adjective ge- indicates possession or provision, so that when it is added to the noun *bird* 'beard' it comes to mean 'having a beard', or 'bearded'. But towards the end of the OE period we find uses of the ge- prefix that do not correspond to these senses, as well as others where the prefixed form shows no semantic distinction from the simple form, as in the verb *gecampian* 'fight', which is identical in meaning to *campian*. Conversion, or zero-derivation is also a very common way of forming new verbs in OE, as in the example of the verb *dagian* 'dawn', derived from the noun *dæg* 'day'.

Compounding was also a very common means of producing new words in OE and we find a range of different types of compound. These include compounds formed from two nouns, as in combinations like *scip* 'ship' + *rāp* 'rope' = 'cable', or *sweord* 'sword' + *freca* 'warrior' = 'sword warrior'. In some instances of noun + noun compounds the first noun is in the genitive case, as in *dægesege* 'daisy', literally 'day's eye'. Distinguishing such compounds from genitive phrases can be difficult, although the clearest examples of genuine compounds are cases where the meaning cannot be deduced from the component parts, as in the case of *daisy*, which is not literally the eye of a day. Adjective + noun compounds are common, as in *haligdæg*, 'holy day', and these types include bahuvrihi compounds such as *heardheort* 'hard heart'. We also find examples of a verbal stem being combined with a noun, as in *bæchūs* 'bakery', and of adverb + noun compounds, e.g. *oferbraw* 'eyebrow'. Adjectival compounds consist of those composed of a noun + adjective, e.g. *dōmgeorn*, literally glory + eager, i.e. eager for glory or *mōdseoc*, literally heart + sick, i.e. sick at heart. Adjectives may also be combined with each other, as in *deorcegrǣg* 'dark grey' and with present and past participles, e.g. *fūlstincende* 'foul stinking' and *hēahgetimbrad* 'high timbered'. Finally, we also find examples of adverb + adjective combinations, as in the formation *ǣrgōd* 'very good'. Compounds were a notable feature of OE poetry and numerous instances survive, particularly to describe common concepts such as warrior, king, sword, horse, armour and battle. Some of these are relatively straightforward, such as *gūþsweord* 'battlesword', or even tautologous, e.g. *gumarinc* 'man + man', while others, known as 'kennings', are more imaginative and metaphorical: e.g. *goldgyfa* 'gold-giver, king'; *hronrād* 'whale road, sea', *ganotes bæth* 'gannet's bath, sea', *gūþscrūd* 'battle clothing, armour'.

5.3 Middle English

Although ME made much greater use of borrowing than OE did as a means of adding to its lexicon, it continued to draw upon the same methods of word formation that were so productive during the OE period. I have already noted above that the large number of OE prefixes began to decay in the late tenth century, and this process of decay continued into the EME period, during which a number died out. Others remained in use but became no longer productive, i.e. no new words were formed using them, as in the case of the be-prefix which is found in ME only in words derived from OE, such as *befalle*, *beginne*, *beteche*, *bethink*. The OE prefix ge-, which was widely used in nouns, adjectives and verbs in OE as we saw above, became unproductive, surviving in a few instances in a reduced form, spelled <i->. It is found in several words inherited from OE, as in *ibrotheren* 'pair of brothers', although this is not used beyond the thirteenth century. There are a handful of new formations using this prefix recorded in the EME period, although they are not found much after 1300. An example is the sole instance of *ibridde*, meaning 'young birds', in the *Owl and the Nightingale*. It did remain as a marker of the past participle up to the late fourteenth century in the southern dialects, e.g. *icomen, idemen*, and even longer in some adverbs, such as *iwis* 'certainly' and *ifere* 'together'.

A number of other affixes did remain productive, but their range of uses changed. If we look at the fortunes of the un- prefix we discussed above we find that its use as a negative was by far the most productive in ME. This use of the un- prefix overlapped in meaning with the prefix an-/on-, as in the verb *onbindan* 'unbind'; the similarity in both sound and meaning led to the un- prefix replacing an-/on entirely. The success of certain prefixes over others, and of certain meanings over others, was partly influenced by the influx of romance affixes. For instance, the success of the un- prefix as the dominant negative prefix was undoubtedly helped by its similarity to French and Latin prefixes in- and im- found in borrowings such as *incomprehensible* and *imprudence*. The in- prefix was productive in ME, although initially it was mostly added to words of romance origin, e.g. *inhonest, indigne*. The overlap between the un- and in- prefixes is demonstrated by the appearance of doublets, comprising both romance bases, e.g. *improfitable/unprofitable, inchaungeable/unchaungeable* and bases of OE origin, e.g. *inunderstondable/ununderstandable*. Many of the un- formations first recorded in ME survive into PDE, such as *unable, uncertain, undeserved* and *unknown*, while others do not, such as *unapt, unkonnynge, unburyed, ungiltyf* and *unfamous*. In addition to its widespread use as a negative prefix, un- continued to be attached to verbs to form the reversal of an action, such as the new ME formations *unclose* 'open', *unbody* 'to leave the body'. The pejorative sense of un- attested in OE formations like *unweder* is much less common, demonstrating the tendency for prefixes to take on more restricted meanings, although ME formations such as *unhap* 'misfortune, bad luck' and *unthank* 'ill will, hostility' may testify to the continued awareness of this sense.

The importance of similarity between native and romance prefixes as a factor in determining the survival of an OE prefix is also demonstrated by the survival of the OE prefix mis- in the ME period. The ME lexicon contains a number of such formations inherited from OE, e.g. *misdeed, mislead*, while others are French loans with an identical prefix, e.g. *mischaunce, misese*. The appearance of the same prefix in inherited and borrowed words meant that it continued to be productive with both inherited and borrowed words, e.g. *misbileve, misdeme, misgoo, misknowing, mislay*; in the case of *mishap* it has been added to a base of ON origin.

The prefix *for-* was added to verbs in OE to add greater intensity to the verb's meaning; inherited words with this prefix continued to be used in ME such as *fordronke* 'completely drunk', *forlost* 'disgraced' and *fortroden* 'trampled upon'. However, the for- prefix became much less productive during the ME period, although new instances did appear, such as the following examples *forwrapped* 'completely wrapped up', *forwelked*, 'withered' or 'shrivelled up' *forsongen*, 'completely exhausted from singing', and *forpassing*, 'surpassing' Most of the examples of these new formations appear as nonce words in the works of Chaucer; that is, they appear just this once in ME, highlighting the marginal status of the for- prefix in ME.

Where French or Latin prefixes did not pair with prefixes inherited from OE, many were found only in loanwords up to the end of the ME period. So the de/des- prefix is found in loanwords from the late thirteenth century but only appears in combination with a native base in the formation *distrust*, first recorded in 1430. The same is true of a number of romance prefixes, such as re-, sub-, super-, mal-, which were all available in loanwords from the late fourteenth and early fifteenth centuries, but did not become productive until the EModE period.

The fate of the OE suffixes is similar to that of the prefixes; of the approximately forty OE suffixes, around thirty survived into ME, while others were adopted from loanwords. For instance, the French ending -*able*, found in loanwords like *reasonable*, was added to English roots to produce new adjectives such as *believable* and *knowable*. Borrowed suffixes were not all of romance origin; the suffix -kin was adopted from Middle Dutch to form diminutives, e.g. *fauntekin* 'little child'; it is particularly common in personal names, e.g. *Jankin* (John + kin) and *Willekin* (William + kin). Another suffix of different origin is the Scandinavian -leik, the cognate of OE *lāc*, used as a further method of forming abstract nouns meaning 'state' or 'condition', as in *hendeleik* 'nobility'. As with the prefixes, some romance suffixes were not productive at all and are only found in borrowed words, e.g. -trice, used to form female agent nouns such as *executrice* 'female executor'. Others were mostly productive only with a romance base, such as the romance suffix -erie, used to form professions or practitioners of a profession, e.g. *chevalrie*, although there are limited instances of its use with an OE base, e.g. *beggerie*.

New compounds that appear in ME represent the same types attested in OE, although it was no longer an important feature of poetic language, especially ones formed by the conjunction of two nouns, e.g. *bagpipe, birthday, schoolmaster*, including examples where the first noun has a genitive inflexion, as found in OE above, e.g. *craftsman*. Other common types are compounds formed from an adjective + noun, e.g. *blackberry, grandfather*, those formed from a verb + noun, e.g. *leap-year*, and noun + noun (where the former is the object of the latter), thus *money-maker, soothsayer, housekeeper*. Bahuvrihi, or exocentric, compounds were also common in ME, especially in nicknames like *pinchpeny* or *gretheved* 'big head'.

5.4 Early Modern English

The huge influx of loanwords in EModE, leading to their prefixes and suffixes becoming productive in English, meant that there were many more affixes available in EModE than there were in ME: a total of around 120 different affixes. The process by which these borrowed affixes became productive was gradual; they were initially added to older loans which had become assimilated into the language, and only subsequently added to more recent loans. The addition of Latinate affixes to Latinate loans that were frequently polysyllabic led to the formation of numerous cumbersome words which were often difficult for speakers who had no knowledge of Latin to analyse.

Among the Latinate prefixes that were introduced during the EModE period are pre-, e.g. *preconception*, counter-, e.g. *counterplot*, dis-, e.g. *discontent*, en-, e.g. *enthrall*. There were many more suffixes than prefixes in EModE; among the many new Latinate suffixes that appear in this period are -al, e.g. *recital*, -ation, e.g. *formalization*, -ance, e.g. *admittance*, -ure, e.g. *exposure*. It is interesting to note that each of these suffixes (along with the native -ing suffix inherited from ME) have the sense of the 'act, cause, result or state' caused by a particular action. This example helps to highlight the considerable overlap in function and meaning of many of the newly borrowed affixes in EModE. A similar degree of overlap is apparent in the borrowed affixes -ate and -fy, which were added to verbs to give the sense of making something become something, as in *facilitate* and *beautify*, a meaning that was already associated with the inherited suffix -en, e.g. *brighten*.

As well as these new prefixes and suffixes being used to form new words, affixes inherited from ME remained productive with new loans. For instance, un- was used to indicate negation of borrowed words, e.g. *unfortunate*, although this kind of mixing of borrowed bases and native affixes, as well as borrowed affixes and native bases, is more common in certain types of texts. It is more common in the works of Shakespeare, for instance, who exploited these types of word formation, than it is in the Authorized Version of the Bible which is much more linguistically conservative. The only loan prefixes that Shakespeare never combines with native bases are de- and pro-, neither of which was very common in EModE. Shakespeare exploited the rich variety of affixes to produce many striking formations, many of which are not found outside his works. Alongside inherited prefixes we often find him employing a recently borrowed Classical equivalent, such as the prefix super in *super-serviceable*, *super-subtle*, alongside the native over-, e.g. *o'erpicturing*. The possibility of selecting from native and foreign bases is also apparent from Shakespeare's use of suffixes. For instance, he used the French derived suffix -ment to coin the words *insultment* and *fleshment* to suggest the action of insulting or fleshing. It is interesting that Shakespeare chose to use the French suffix -ment rather than the native suffix -ing, given that the latter was the more common way of forming nouns from verbs denoting actions. In fact he could have used the Latin suffix -ance, giving *insultance* or, instead of forming a new word, he might have employed a loanword, such as *insult*, or *insultation*, both of which were already part of the EModE lexicon (Nevalainen, 2001).

Despite the huge range of prefixes and suffixes that were available during the EModE period, it is interesting to note that native affixes remained more common than borrowed ones: the most commonly used suffixes were -ness and -er, while -ed and -y are the most frequently attested adjective suffixes.

Zero-derivation, or conversion, was also common in EModE, especially in the production of verbs from nouns or adjectives. Verbs formed this way often have the sense of causation, as in the example given above of the verb *bottle*, which has the sense of causing something to be put into a bottle. A number of new conversions are first recorded in Shakespeare's works indicating the usefulness of this means of word formation; examples include *stranger* 'turn into a stranger', *dumb* 'make dumb'. As with the examples of affixation discussed above, often these conversions overlap in meaning with existing words, so that we might wonder why it was necessary to employ this method of word formation. For instance, the verb *dumb* has a similar meaning to the verb *silence*; the distinction between the two is perhaps one of register, especially given that one is a native word and the other a loanword.

Compounding remained a productive method of word formation during the EModE period, with noun + noun combinations being the most common types, as is also true of PDE. These are discussed and exemplified by William Bullokar in an interesting section in his *Pamphlet for Grammar* of 1586 (quoted in Nevalainen, 2006). Bullokar begins by including a passage which gives numerous examples of types of compounds:

> On an erth-bank ner medow-ground, I saw a hors-comb ly, Which I browht intoo a hors-mil that a ston wal stood nih, And fynding thaer an elmen plank, I sowht for a wood-betl And woodn wedges, but found nawht, sauing a laten-ketl.

He then gives the same passage again with paraphrases showing the meaning of these various compound words:

> On a bank of erth or erthn bank, ner ground for medow, I saw a comb for a hors ly, which I browht intoo a mil with hors, that stood nih a stonen wal, or wal of ston, and fynding thaer an elm-plank, or plank of elm, I sowht for a betl for wood, and wedges of wood, but found nothing, sauing a ketl of laten.

This passage gives many examples of noun + noun compounds, demonstrating its prevalence, e.g. *erth-bank*, *medow-ground*, *hors-comb*. But there are also many examples of adjective + noun compounds such as *elmen plank*, *wooden wedges*. It is also common to find adjectives consisting of noun + adjective combinations in EModE, such as *fireproof*, *world-wide*, or noun + past participle: *frost-bitten*, *heart-felt*. Shakespeare exploited these various compounding possibilities extensively. Adjectives formed on the nominal base *heart* were a particular favourite; there are over twenty examples in his works. Some of these are traditional ones, such as *hard-hearted*, *tender-hearted*, while others are first recorded in his works: *maiden-hearted*, *marble-hearted*, *pitiful-hearted*.

5.5 Borrowing

The PDE lexicon consists of words from a variety of different sources: OE, ON, French and Latin, as well as numerous other languages with which English has come into contact throughout its history. The words inherited from OE comprise the basis of ME vocabulary and many of these words survive into PDE. These include many core vocabulary items such as the kinship terms *father*, *mother*, *brother* and *sister*. Other words have been introduced as a result of borrowing, a term used by linguists to describe the process whereby a language adopts a word from another language, though it is not an entirely appropriate one as the word is, of course, never returned. The kinds of words borrowed from these languages differ according to the kind of contact, and the subsequent interaction between the donor and recipient languages. In many cases borrowing is a straightforward process in which a new word is adopted to express a new concept. However, there are also instances where new words are borrowed whose meanings overlap with existing words in the language. In response to this overlap, the meaning of one or both words may change to create a distinction or a distinction in connotation or register may be introduced. The first process is demonstrated in the case of the English words *skirt* and *shirt*. The word *skirt* was adopted from ON and had the same meaning as the OE *shirt*, with both words deriving ultimately from the same Germanic root. Once the ON word was borrowed it developed a different meaning to distinguish it from the existing word *shirt*, a distinction still found in PDE. The second process is demonstrated by the adoption of the French verb *regard* in the ME period. This verb's meaning overlapped considerably with the existing verb *look at* and was distinguished according to register rather than meaning. This register distinction is still found in PDE, as can be seen from the difference in formality between the two sentences: 'Look at the blackboard!' and 'Regard the blackboard!'

Because of these distinctions between words that stand out as foreign and those which are fully assimilated into the language, it is customary for linguists to distinguish three different categories of loanwords. A Gastwort is a loanword which retains the original spelling and pronunciation of the original and so remains unassimilated into English. Examples in PDE include the French loanword *milieu* and the German loan *Zeitgeist*. It is a feature of these words that they do not become productive in the language, that is they are not used to form new words. A Fremdwort is one which has been partially assimilated into English; a good example of this is the noun *garage*, which retains its French pronunciation [gæɑːʒ] in some accents, while others employ an English pronunciation [gærɪdʒ]. Such words can be productive, as in the case of *garage*, which, since the early twentieth century, has been used as a verb meaning 'put a car in a garage'. A Lehnwort is a word that has been fully assimilated into the language and is no longer distinguished as a borrowing, like the noun *fruit*. This word is an Old French borrowing but one which is now totally assimilated into English and which has been used to coin new formations such as *fruity*, *fruitful* and *fruitless*. As well as these three major types of loan translation there is a more specialized category, known as calques. Calques differ from loanwords in being translations from another language rather than borrowings, as in the English word *superman*, a translation of the German *Übermensch*. In the following section of this chapter we will investigate the various ways in which English has employed these methods of borrowing throughout its history.

5.6 Old English

OE relied comparatively little on borrowing to supplement its lexicon and much more on internal processes of word formation. There were, however, a small number of loanwords in OE, most of which came from the Latin language. The influence of Latin was felt in three separate stages: the first wave of loans was adopted on the continent, before the Anglo-Saxon invasions, the second set of Latin borrowings occurred during the early period of settlement, while the third set is connected to the process of Christianization which took place in the early seventh century.

The first set of Latin loans are found in a number of the Germanic dialects and are the result of contact between Germanic tribes and the Romans on the continent. Because of the nature of the contact between these peoples a large proportion of these words relate to trade, the military and Roman civilization. It was during this period that the Germanic dialects adopted words like *wīn* 'wine' (Latin *vinum*), *ceaster* 'city' (Latin *castra*), *strǣt* 'street' (Latin *via strata*). These words derive not from Classical Latin, but from a vulgar Latin spoken by ordinary Roman soldiers. The second period of Latin influence may have come directly from the Latin spoken by the Romanized Britons, or perhaps from the continent. Latin words adopted during this period comprise a similar collection of words relating to everyday life, such as terms associated with cooking and agriculture, although there are also some religious words, e.g. *munuc* 'monk' (Latin *monachus*), *mynster* 'monastery' (Latin *monasterium*), *mæsse* 'mass'. During the third period, following the Christianization of England, we find a substantial focus on religion and learning. Most of these words are learned and were probably found exclusively in writing, e.g. *apostol* 'apostle'(Latin *apostulus*); *abbod* 'abbot' (Latin *abbadem*); *scōl* 'school' (Latin *scola*). In the tenth century there was another wave of borrowings from Classical Latin as a result of the Benedictine reform, although many of these were technical terms that remained as Fremdwörter and were not integrated into the native language. Their foreign status was emphasized by the preservation of their foreign spellings and structure, as is evident in the case of the later OE loan *magister* (Latin *magister*), which may be contrasted with the earlier loan *mægester*, derived from the same Latin word. As with the previous example, a number of these Classical borrowings replaced existing OE formations, such as *grammaticcræft* 'grammar', designed to replace the native word *stæfcræft*.

A more complex kind of borrowing is known as a semantic borrowing, where it is the meaning of a Latin word that is borrowed rather than the word itself. This is well exemplified by the influence of the Latin word *pastor*. The primary meaning of this word was 'shepherd', but it could also be used in religious contexts to refer to God. Rather than borrowing the word *pastor*, OE adopted this additional meaning so that the meaning of the OE word *hierde* 'shepherd' was extended to refer to God. A similar example of a semantic borrowing, where the link between the two words is less apparent, is the OE word *cniht* 'child, servant' which took on the meaning of the Latin noun *discipulus* 'disciple'. This method was particularly common in religious vocabulary as it meant that a previously pagan usage could be fully replaced by a Christian one. For example, the OE word *god* 'that which is invoked', and its plural form *godas*, was used to refer to the pagan deities. When introducing the Anglo-Saxons to the Christian concept of a single deity, rather than introduce the Latin word *Deus* the Christian missionaries simply employed the singular form of the extant word *god*. As a consequence the singular form of the noun came to be used exclusively to refer to the Christian God, while its plural form continued to refer to pagan deities. A further distinction that arose as a result of this process of dissimulation was that the singular noun *god* was accorded masculine gender, while the plural noun was neuter (Strang, 1970). The process of Christianization also led to the introduction of a number of calques, such as the rendering of the Latin word for 'trinity', *trinitas*, by the OE translation *priness* and the Latin *evangelii* by the OE *gōdspell*, and the use of *mildheort* for Latin *misericors*.

Compared to the number of Latin loans the influence of Celtic upon OE is extremely small. This is the result of the low status that the Celts occupied following the Anglo-Saxon invasions. Following these invasions Celts took refuge in the extreme areas of the west and the north of the country, areas which have been Celtic speaking until the present day or, in the case of Cornwall, until relatively recently. Where there was contact between Celtic speakers and Anglo-Saxons the balance of power was firmly in favour of the Anglo-Saxons, for whom the Celts served as slaves. Because of this the majority of Celtic influence is found in place names and river names, such as the common river name Avon which is a Celtic word for 'river' (cf. Welsh *afon*). Having said this, a small number of Celtic loans date back to the continental period, e.g. *rīce* 'rule, reign, empire', while some others were borrowed after the period of settlement, e.g. *dunn* 'dark coloured, grey' and *broc* 'badger'. A few additional Celtic words were adopted from Irish missionaries during the process of Christianization, e.g. *drȳ* 'magician, sorcerer' (Old Irish *drui*, pl. *druid*), although, because of their association with Christianity, many of these are ultimately of Latin origin, e.g. *ancor* 'hermit, anchorite', (Old Irish *anchara*).

There are a number of Scandinavian loans in OE, but not nearly as many as we might expect given the degree of contact between Anglo-Saxons and Scandinavians during the extensive period of invasion and settlement. Many more Scandinavian loanwords appear for the first time in the ME period, several centuries after the Viking invasions. The reason for this is that a large percentage of the OE written records that survive were copied in LWS (see Chapter 3), a variety based on the dialect of Wessex. The areas of Viking settlement were principally the East Midlands and the North and as a consequence words borrowed from Scandinavian did not filter into the written language. During the ME period, following the demise of LWS and the emergence of writing systems closely reflecting local usage, Scandinavian words began to appear in the written records, although they were doubtless used in the spoken language during the OE period. Similarities between the Scandinavian languages and OE, both are Germanic languages deriving from the same ancestor, may well have encouraged the transfer of words from one language to the other. The contrast in status between the Scandinavian and Celtic languages is also instructive: where the Celts occupied a lowly role in Anglo-Saxon society, the Vikings were the invaders, subsequently settling and integrating into the existing society.

The earliest examples of ON borrowings are in place names, which help to show the level of interaction between OE and ON during this early period. Place names that contain the Scandinavian elements *by* 'village' or *thorp* 'farm', such as Grimsby and Scunthorpe, attest to this early influence of ON. Because of their status as cognates, languages deriving from the same ancestor, it is not always immediately obvious whether a word is of OE or ON origin. A major pronunciation difference between OE and ON meant that words beginning with /sk/, /g/ and /k/ in OE are ON in origin, although this is not always clear from the OE spelling, e.g. *giefan* 'give' which could indicate a pronunciation with /g/ or /j/ (see the discussion of spelling and pronunciation in Chapter 4). Where both OE and ON words have identical spellings, the meaning can help to distinguish them. Scandinavian loanwords recorded in OE tend to belong to specialized registers, especially seafaring and military terms associated particularly with the Viking invasions, e.g. *lið* 'fleet' (ON *lið*), *cnearr* 'small ship' (ON *knǫrr*), *lipsmenn* 'sailors'. The influence of the Vikings on the OE legal system is apparent from loanwords like *grið* 'truce'(ON *grið*), *husting* 'tribunal, court'(ON *húsþing*), *utlaga* 'outlaw', and their relatively high status in OE society is apparent from the adoption of terms of rank, such as *husbonda* 'householder'(ON *bóndi*), *eorl* 'nobleman' (ON *jarl*).

5.7 Middle English

In the ME period the main source of new words was the borrowing of words from other languages; partly the result of increased contact with other languages. As we noted above, it is during the ME period that the impact of the Scandinavian languages on the English lexicon becomes apparent, although it is likely that many ON words were first borrowed in the OE period but remained part of the spoken, rather than the written, language. Because of the similarities between ON and ME, and the extended period of Viking settlement in England, ME shows the adoption of a considerable number of words borrowed from ON, although even in ME the effects are delayed. Even the *Ormulum*, a text written *c.* 1200 in the East Midlands, an area of dense Norse settlement, contains only approximately 120 loans in a total of 20,000 lines. Outside the focal areas of Scandinavian settlement, the number of loans is even slighter: there are around 70 in the south-west Midland text *Ancrene Riwle* and less than forty in Laʒamon's *Brut*, written in the same area. While it is clear that this distribution is partly the result of dialect distinctions, it is also likely that ON words were not considered appropriate for use in the literary register. Many of the words derived from ON in ME were everyday words which became thoroughly assimilated into the English lexicon. These words often describe concepts which are basic to English language and culture, words like *egg, husband, knife, leg, take, thursday, ugly, want, window*. We noted above that a major pronunciation difference between ON and OE means that many of the English words which begin with /sk-/ are derived from ON, e.g. *sky, skin, skill*; many of these words first appear during the ME period. The interaction between ON and ME also led to the adoption into ME of the ON third person plural pronouns, *they, their* and *them*, which were borrowed to remedy a lack of distinctiveness in the OE derived paradigm (see further Chapter 6), and the present plural form of the verb *be*: *are* is also of ON derivation. There were more examples of grammatical words borrowed from ON in ME that have since been lost: *oc* 'but', *heþen* 'hence', *fra* 'from', *summ* 'as', *wheþen* 'whence', *umb-* 'about'. The adoption of ON vocabulary in ME varied according to geography, reflecting the patterns of Viking settlement in the Anglo-Saxon period. A result of this is that the adoption of ON borrowings differs according to dialect, with the dialects of the north and East Midlands showing the greatest number of ON loans. Thus ON borrowings such as *slik* 'such', *starn* 'star', and *kirk* 'church' are features of northern and eastern dialects, while the southern and western dialects continued to use the OE equivalents *swich*, *sterre* and *chirch*. This distinction is still found in PDE, where larger numbers of ON loans survive in the Northern dialects than in the standard language, e.g. *laik* 'play', *gowk* 'fool', *lug* 'ear'.

The late appearance of ON words in our written sources makes it difficult to distinguish between words derived from Swedish, Norwegian and Danish, though Danish forms are more common in the East Midlands dialects, and Norwegian loans more common in the north and west. This reflects a distinction in patterns of settlement which had an important bearing on the future of the standard language. As this standard was based upon the East Midlands dialects it was the Danish forms that were adopted.

Another important feature of Norse influence on the English lexicon is in the phrasal verbs: verbs followed by prepositions or adverbs. The earliest recorded examples of these verbs are found in the *Peterborough Chronicle*, e.g. *gyfen up, faren mid, leten up, tacen to*. Also of Norse influence is the use of the verbal operator *get*, as in our modern idioms *get up, get away, get out*; this feature is particularly common in northern texts such as Cur*sor Mundi*.

Compared to the impact of other languages upon English during the ME period, the number of words derived from Latin is rather small, and words themselves tend to be associated with specialized domains such as religion and learning, as witnessed by words like *scripture*, *history* and *allegory*. The use of Latin alongside French in government, the law and administration led to the adoption of a number of key terms from Latin, such as *client, conviction* and *executor*. Latin and French are of course closely related, in that French is ultimately derived from Latin, and this means that many ME loans can appear similar to both Latin and French originals, making it difficult to determine which the immediate source was. Even where there are differences in form, these could have been the result of changes made to a Latin word when it entered French, or when it was borrowed directly into English. One instance of such a difficulty is presented by the verb *enclinen*, which may be spelled either *enclinen* or *inclinen* in ME, making it difficult to determine whether it derives from French *encliner* or from Latin *inclinare*.

In the fifteenth century a style of writing emerged known as aureate diction, a stylistic mode particularly associated with the poetic works of Chaucer's follower John Lydgate. Aureate diction aimed to create a highly artificial and elevated style which employed polysyllabic Latinate words, like *superaboundaunt*, to create a linguistic register sufficiently grand to be employed in liturgical contexts and to venerate the Virgin Mary. While this style was artificial and poetic, and many of the words introduced in such works have not been adopted into English, it does prefigure the process of classical borrowing which occurred on a much larger scale in the EModE period, as we will see below.

The largest number of borrowed words adopted during the ME period is from French, a consequence of the Norman Conquest and the replacement of Anglo-Saxon culture and government with that of the Norman conquerors. Borrowing of words from French during the ME period can be divided into two main stages. The first stage, which occurred immediately after the Conquest, witnessed the adoption of words taken directly from the Norman French dialect. Words adopted during this stage generally relate to concepts of particular importance to the Normans in establishing their government, and therefore include words such as *justice, chancellor, prison, noble, crime, court*. The *Peterborough Chronicle* has a number of specialized French words that were adopted into English during this first stage of borrowing, many of which are associated with the law, e.g. *tenserie* 'a form of taxation', *werre* 'war', *pais* 'peace', *iustice* 'justice', *acorden* 'come to agreement'. Other French words attested in the *Peterborough Chronicle* are ecclesiastical, e.g. *pasches* 'Easter', *miracle, canonie* 'canon', *capitele* 'chapter', *clerc* 'scholar', while others concern aristocratic titles, e.g. *duc, cuntesse, emperice, rente*. Some French borrowings indicate the need for terms to describe new concepts, such as the word *tenserie* which has to be explained by the chronicler. Yet the majority of these loans do not represent new concepts but were chosen because of their higher status which was felt to be appropriate for the literary register.

The origin of these words in the Norman dialect of French, rather than that of the Central French dialect, is apparent in the form in which some words were borrowed. For example, the ME *werre* 'war' is derived from Norman French *werre* rather than the standard French form *guerre*. In other cases both Norman French and Central French forms have been adopted into English, as in the case of *warranty* and *guarantee*, where the former term has become restricted to specialized legal contexts, and other pairs such as *wile* and *guile*, *warden* and *guardian*, *reward* and *regard*.

The second stage of borrowing from French saw the adoption of words from the Central French dialect which are not restricted to any particular linguistic domain. Given that French speakers and French culture were perceived as being socially desirable throughout this period, it is not surprising that these words generally relate to refined and elevated areas of English culture, including the arts, e.g. *paint, music, verse*; fashion, e.g. *robe, gown*; and food e.g. *mutton, beef*. This second stage of borrowing witnessed the greatest number of French borrowings, with the flood of French loanwords peaking around 1400, and then dropping off in the fifteenth century. While many of the French words borrowed in the ME period were stylistically elevated, a number were also quickly assimilated into the language. This process of assimilation can be observed by noting the extent to which French loanwords were subsequently subjected to the English processes of compounding and affixation described in the previous section. For example, the word *gentle* is a French borrowing which was combined with other English words to produce new terms, such as *gentleman* and *gentlewoman*, while many French adjectives formed adverbs through the addition of the English ending -ly, e.g. *courteously*.

The profound way in which French affected ME vocabulary is also demonstrated by the replacement of OE words with French synonyms, especially in core concepts such as kinship terms, e.g. *uncle, aunt, nephew, niece* and *cousin* are all of French origin. The number and nature of French borrowings in this period often varies according to the type of text. Courtly literary works tend to employ many more French loans, and this is particularly true of works which are translations of French originals.

By contrast with the considerable impact of French on the English lexicon, the influence of Celtic on ME is very small. However, as with the ON words discussed above, it is likely that many more Celtic words were in use in the spoken language but were not considered to be appropriate for use in the written register. Celtic words which are recorded from this period include words associated with Celtic culture, such as *bard* and *clan*, as well as topographic terms, such as *crag* and *glen*. Trading links with the Low Countries led to the introduction of a number of words of Middle Dutch origin into ME. These words are generally concerned with trade and shipping and include *skipper, pump, bung, grot* and *tub*, although there are some brewing and drinking terms too: *bouse* 'to drink deeply', *gyle* 'a batch of ale brewed at one time', *kilderkin* 'cask'.

5.8 Early Modern English

The EModE period is the period in the history of English in which the vocabulary expanded at its greatest rate. During this period something in the region of 12,000 new words were introduced into English. Where the OE period relied almost exclusively on internal methods of word formation to augment its lexicon, the EModE period made far greater use of borrowing as a means of enriching the lexicon. Borrowing was responsible for introducing more new words than affixation, compounding and conversion put together. The most common category of loanword during this period is the noun, followed by adjectives and then verbs. The number of new borrowings grew during the sixteenth century, peaking during the period from 1570 and 1630 and then tailing off in the middle of the sixteenth century. It is important to stress that this large figure includes those words that were used just once or twice, as well as many words which were used throughout the period but which have not survived into PDE. This was a period that celebrated lexical innovation and so we find numerous nonce words, words that appear just once in the historical record.

The majority of words introduced during this period are of Latin origin. While many Latin loanwords were adopted during the ME period, many of these entered the language via French rather than directly from Classical Latin. During the EModE period these loans came directly from Latin, creating a number of doublets where the same Latin word appears twice: once in a form borrowed from French in the ME period and again in a Latin form adopted during the EModE period. For example, the verb *count* was borrowed from French *conter* in the fourteenth century, although its ultimate root is the Latin verb *computare*. The same verb is borrowed again during the sixteenth century, this time directly from Latin in the form *compute*. Other examples of this process include the ME *poor* (Old French *povre*) and EModE *pauper* (Latin *pauper*) and ME *sure* (Old French *seur*) and EModE *secure* (Latin *securus*). We saw in Chapter 4 how a number of French borrowings were respelled to reflect a Latin etymology, and this respect for Latin spelling meant that many Latin loanwords were adopted with their Latin endings, such as *folio* and *proviso*, in which the -o ending indicates the ablative case. In other examples we find verb endings preserved, as in *exit*, *ignoramus*, as well as entire verb phrases in *facsimile*, *factotum*. Despite this desire to preserve the Latin appearance of loanwords, some words did lose their endings to make them fit better with English morphological patterns, e.g. *immature* from Latin *immaturus*, *exotic* from *exoticus*.

While Latin was by far the largest source of new words, a number of borrowings came from French, although, as with the ME period, it is not always possible to determine whether a Latin loan came directly from Latin or indirectly via French.

In some cases the form itself shows the direction of the borrowing. So, for instance, in the mid-sixteenth century the two verbs *prejudge* and *prejudicate* were borrowed. *Prejudge* is clearly from the French *prejuger*, while *prejudicate* was borrowed directly from the Latin *prejudicare*. Presumably the similarity in the meanings of these two verbs meant that only one was required and it was the French loan that survived. But in other cases it is simply not possible to determine from the form of the word whether it is derived from

Latin or French. The noun *proclivity*, meaning 'inclination', is first recorded in 1591. The *OED* gives it a Latin etymon, deriving it from Latin *proclivitas* 'tendency, propensity', although it also compares the similar French form *proclivité*. French loanwords adopted towards the end of the seventeenth and into the eighteenth centuries are much easier to identify, as these often remained deliberately unassimilated. During this period French manners and culture were very fashionable, leading to the adoption of French words with their native spelling and even pronunciation intact. In most cases the words that were borrowed during this period still retain their French spelling and pronunciation in PDE, e.g. *repartee, liaison, faux pas* and *beau*. The fashion for such words among the nobility was condemned by Addison and Johnson; it subsequently died out following the rise in prominence of the middle class and the corresponding fall in prestige of the nobility following the French Revolution.

A much smaller group of loanwords entered EModE from other European languages, such as Italian, Spanish and Dutch. The majority of these borrowings relate to trade between Britain and these countries during this period. Some Italian loans include commodities such as *parmesan* and *artichoke*, as well as architectural terms like *balcony* and *cupola* and words relating to the arts, e.g. *stanza, violin*. Spanish loans reflect trading related to colonization, e.g. *anchovy, apricot, banana, cocoa, potato, tobacco*, while Dutch words include *guilder, excise, hose*. Non-European loans reflect travel further afield and include Persian and Arabic words, borrowed via Turkish, e.g. *caftan, sherbert, yogurt, turban, divan, caravan*, Indian loans, e.g. *cot, pundit, bungalow, dungaree, pukka, shampoo* and others derived from North American Indian languages, e.g. *raccoon, moccasin, moose, wigwam, skunk*.

The reason for lexical borrowing on this vast scale is connected to the status of the vernacular and its appropriateness as a literary language. During the sixteenth century numerous writers raised concerns about the sufficiency of the vernacular as a vehicle for the translation of authoritative works such as the Bible and the Classics. There were two particular problems that were identified by these writers: the lack of specialized terminology and the lack of sufficiently elevated vocabulary. During the ME period, as we have seen, religious and scientific texts were written in French and Latin and so the English language had not developed the stylistic resources of a literary and scientific language. To remedy this situation EModE writers set about enriching the English language by increasing its vocabulary via lexical borrowing. The reason that borrowing was favoured over word formation is connected to the kinds of literary activity commonly engaged in during this period. The particular focus on translation of texts composed in Latin and Greek into English led to the borrowing of numerous words from these languages, because the simplest solution for a translator faced with a classical word with no English equivalent was to borrow the classical word into English. Borrowing of this kind is largely functional, in that it helps to supply words to express concepts where relevant words are lacking.

But not all borrowing during this period was motivated by these strictly practical concerns. Some writers chose to import classical words where English already had an equivalent word. Borrowings of this kind are stylistic, in that they were influenced by a respect for the classical languages and a belief that classical loans helped to create a more elevated stylistic register. Writers who favoured the adoption of numerous loanwords are known as 'neologizers', because of their support for the use of neologisms, or 'new words'. The neologizers had their opponents, who objected to the kind of stylistic borrowing on the grounds that it was unnecessary and ostentatious. Others felt that the introduction of large numbers of classical words into English was unhelpful for those who had not had the benefits of a classical education and thus were not literate in Latin and Greek. Still others objected on the grounds that many of these classical borrowings were unnecessary, given that they were often borrowed alongside English equivalents. This group of writers, concerned with keeping English free of unnecessary foreign borrowings, is known as the 'Purists', and it includes scholars like Sir John Cheke, who wished to see the language preserved as 'pure, unmixt and unmangeled with borowing of other tunges'. The Purists believed that the resources of the English language were sufficient to fill any gaps in the lexicon. To demonstrate this Sir John Cheke made a translation of the Gospel of St Matthew relying exclusively on words formed from native resources using traditional methods of word formation and loan translations, both typical features of OE. Instead of *resurrection* Cheke used the word *gainrising*, he preferred *biwordes* to *parables*, *mooned* for *lunatic*, *onwriting* for *superscription*, *hundreder* for *centurion*, *washing* for *baptism*. As well as forming new words in this way, some writers deliberately revived archaic, poetic words, such as those that had been used in the ME period but had since died out. The most important member of this group, known as the Archaizers, was the poet Edmund Spenser who reintroduced a number of words used by ME literary writers like Chaucer, words like *doom*, *natheles*, as well as words which had only survived in dialect use, like the Northern dialect form of 'much' *mickle*. As well as these revivals of obsolete words, the Archaizers employed new derivations from archaic poetic words. Examples of this process include the adjective *drear*, a shortening of the OE *dreary* which first occurs in Milton, and *baneful*, derived from OE *bana* and first recorded in Spenser's *Shepherds' Calendar*. This was a small and specialized movement with few followers and many critics. Perhaps the most famous of its opponents was Ben Jonson, who wrote of Spenser that 'in affecting the ancients [he] writ no language'. One of Spenser's supporters, who signs himself E.K., praised his efforts to restore 'to their rightfull heritage such good and naturall English words as have ben long time out of use and almost cleane disherited'. The Purists ridiculed the introduction of learned loanwords purely for stylistic reasons, labelling them 'inkhorn terms' and the debate that this gave rise to is known as the 'Inkhorn Controversy'.

The ridiculing of the use of inkhorn terms is well exemplified by Thomas Wilson's *The Arte of Rhetorique* (1553), in which Wilson quotes from a letter supposedly written by a Lincolnshire man addressed to one of the Lord Chancellor's gentlemen. The letter is clearly a fabrication, designed to satire the pompous style associated with the Neologizers. The letter begins as follows:

> Pondering, expending, and revoluting with my selfe, your ingent affabilitie, and ingenious capacity for mundaine affaires: I cannot but celebrate, & extol your magnifical dexteritie above all other. For how could you have adepted such illustrate prerogative, and dominicall superioritie, if the fecunditie of your ingenie had not been so fertile and wonderfull pregnant.

Many of the words Wilson uses in this fictional letter were recent borrowings and many were used only very infrequently. These new borrowings are clearly Latinate in origin, as in *expending* (Latin *expendere* 'weigh up'), *ingent* (Latin *ingens* 'huge'), *adepted* (Latin *adeptus* 'attained'), *ingenie* (Latin *ingenium* 'mind').

Shakespeare referred to this controversy in his play *Love's Labour's Lost*, in which certain characters employ Latin words and phrases and Latinate inkhorn terms purely to show off their great learning and eloquence. One of the characters, called Don Armado, a man of 'fire-new words', uses the affected vocabulary of the neologizers. The pedant, Holofernes, is clearly intended to poke fun at the overuse of classical loanwords, as is the curate, Nathaniel, who makes note of his master's vocabulary so that he can adopt them himself. The following exchange demonstrates the highly artificial nature of Holofernes's vocabulary and the attempts by Nathaniel to adopt a similar register himself:

Holofernes: Satis quod sufficit.
Nathaniel: I praise God for you, sir. Your reasons at dinner have been sharp and sententious; pleasant without scurrility, witty without affection, audacious without impudency, learned without opinion and strange without heresy. I did converse this quondam day with a companion of the King's, who is intituled, nominated, or called, Don Adriano de Armado.
Holofernes: Novi hominem tanquam te. His humour is lofty, his discourse peremptory, his tongue filed, his eye ambitious, his

> gait majestical and his general behaviour vain, ridiculous and thrasonical. He is too picked, too spruce, too affected, too odd, as it were, too peregrinate, as I may call it.
>
> Nathaniel: A most singular and choice epithet (Draws out his table-book)
>
> (Love's Labour's Lost, 5.1.1–16)

Here we witness the pedant dropping Latin words and phrases into his speech to sound impressive, as well as using polysyllabic Latinate loan words. Nathaniel's repetition of 'intituled, nominated, or called' highlights the importance of register as a factor governing the introduction and use of loanwords. These three verbs have the same meaning but their different etymologies mean that they belong to different registers. The French loan *intituled* and the Latin *nominated* clearly belong to the higher stylistic register, while *called*, an ON loan that was first adopted in the EME period, has no such lofty pretensions. Despite satirizing the neologizers in this way Shakespeare himself drew extensively on recent borrowing, while many of the loanwords he used are first recorded in his plays. This shows that, while extreme forms of borrowing could appear ridiculous, borrowing was a necessary and commonplace feature of EModE writing. We have seen above how common borrowing was during the ME period, and the EModE period simply continued this trend.

The Purists were clearly the minority voice, with most writers recognizing the merits of borrowing, a practice that was even found in Latin and Greek. While borrowings may appear foreign and unusual at first, they soon become familiar through use, as we saw with French loans in the ME period. This was acknowledged by Richard Mulcaster who wrote that 'all strange things seme great novelties, and hard of entertainment at their first arrivall, till theie be acquainted: but after acquaintance theie be verie familiar, and easie to entreat'. By the end of the sixteenth century so many new words had already been borrowed that the Inkhorn controversy was effectively silenced. In the early seventeenth century the debate was refocused on the restriction of loanwords to those that were strictly necessary. As a consequence many writers felt the need to justify some of the loanwords they used, so that George Puttenham argued that it would be impossible to do without words like *scientific, method, compendious* and *figurative*. But Puttenham's views have not always been borne out by history, as some of the words he claimed were invaluable, such as *assubtiling* have not survived and so evidently were not as necessary as he thought.

A number of new borrowings that were common in EModE but then subsequently dropped out of the language, such as the word *salutiferous*, a Latin borrowing meaning 'conducive to health'. The *OED* notes that this word was 'very common in the 17th century', although it has since fallen out of use

entirely. The reasons for the loss of such words are not always easy to determine, although some may have appeared too learned, or their meanings overlapped with existing words. So the loss of the polysyllabic *salutiferous* may be
linked to the adoption of the simpler loanword *salubrious*, another Latin loan,
first recorded in the sixteenth century and used with a similar range of meanings. The existence of a native term with an equivalent meaning, *wholesome*,
whose meaning was more transparent to English speakers, meant that the
polysyllabic loanword was not required and so it eventually became obsolete.
The preference for a single word rather than two words with a similar set of
meanings is also demonstrated by the verbs *expede* and *expedite*. Both were
derived from the same Latin root, *expedire*, in the seventeenth century, both
with the same meaning, but only *expedite* has survived in the standard language. Despite its similar form to *impede*, a word with the opposite meaning,
the form *expede* has only survived as a Scottish legal term.

5.9 Semantic change

In the previous section we examined the way that the English language has
borrowed words from other languages with which it has come into contact
throughout its history. While in many cases borrowing simply introduces a
new word to describe a new concept, there are many other instances where
the interaction between a borrowed word and other words is more complex.
As we noted above, words are frequently polysemous, so that a new word
is likely to overlap to some extent with others in the same 'semantic field'.
The result of this interaction is that one or more of the words in this semantic field change its meaning, a process known as 'semantic change'. Like all
types of linguistic change that we have discussed so far in this book, semantic
change is an inevitable feature of a living language; in fact the lexicon is the
most unstable part of a linguistic system and the most prone to variation and
change. Despite this, semantic change is frequently lamented by commentators who complain about the way that words are being misused. The reason
for such complaints is that there is a common misapprehension that words
have a single 'true' meaning that has been corrupted through misuse. This
view is linked to the belief that the etymology of a word gives its true meaning, which has since been lost as a result of misuse and misunderstanding.
This view is apparent from the word *etymology* itself, which is derived from
the Greek word *etymos* meaning 'true'. This view, however, is a myth: there is
no such thing as a single, correct meaning. Polysemy, or multiple meanings,
is extremely common and some words have numerous meanings. Take a simple word like the verb *cut*, for instance, which has 65 different senses listed
in the *OED*. As a result of this multiplicity of senses, the meanings of many

words overlap creating 'synonymy'. The principal meaning of the verb *cut* is 'to make incision in or into', a meaning which clearly overlaps with the core meanings of other verbs, such as *slice*: 'to cut into or through with a sharp instrument' or *chop*: 'to cut with a blow'. So we could use any of the three verbs to describe cutting down a tree. But while these words evidently share a similar core sense, there are distinctions to be made in the nature of the incision and the type of instrument being used. While we could *cut* or *slice* a cake, we would never *chop* it. We can *cut* the grass, but would never *slice* or *chop* it. So while they are broadly synonymous they are not exact synonyms. In addition to these fine shades of meanings, these words also have a variety of supplementary senses that are specific to these words alone. There are specialized uses, such as the geometric sense of *cut*, meaning 'intersect', or the golfing sense of *slice*, 'hitting the ball so that it curves to the right' and the cricketing use of *chop*, 'bringing the bat down heavily and quickly on the ball'. In addition to these meanings these words have figurative senses, such as in the expressions *cut to the heart* and *get the chop*. Finally we must also be aware of dialectal differences: words may have different senses in different dialects. A northern form of *chop*, *chap*, is used in Scots to mean 'knock', as in the expression: *chap on the door*, while in the United States *cut* can be used to mean 'dilute' and *slice* can replace *look at* in the expression *no matter how you slice it*. These three examples of verbs with shared meanings help to make the point that, while their senses overlap, they are by no means exact synonyms. If we broaden our discussion further to encompass other verbs that share the primary sense of making an incision with a sharp object, then we find a large number of other verbs are available. But, as before, these verbs can be distinguished more precisely in terms of their meaning, the nature of the instrument and the type of blow used. They may also be distinguished in terms of their use, so that a surgeon will *amputate* a leg rather than *chop it off*, *lance* a boil rather than *slice* it and make an *incision* rather than a *cut*.

What this example has taught us is that there is no such thing as exact synonymy; words have numerous associations: stylistic, sociolinguistic, dialectal, generational, figurative and metaphorical, which allow us to make fine-grained distinctions between members of a semantic field. We have also seen the extent of polysemy that exists between words, and the frequency with which one word's senses overlap with those of other words.

Much work on semantic change has been concerned with trying to categorize the ways in which words change their meanings, although, as we will see, many examples resist any simple categorization. But let us begin with the more straightforward examples which exhibit some of the clearest instances of particular types of semantic change.

One obvious way in which a word's meaning may change is the direct result of cultural innovation or social change. So, for instance, the word *caste* in OE referred to a 'fortified village', but in early ME technological and social changes led to its use to refer to a 'stone-built fortress'. Similarly the introduction of the chivalric code in the ME period through direct contact with prestigious French culture led to changes in the use of the word *knight*. This word derives from the OE *cniht*, which meant 'boy' or 'servant'; during the ME period it was used to describe the military servant of a king or nobleman, or a warrior serving a lady, either in a battle or in a tournament. Such figures were the heroes of numerous legendary stories, such as those associated with King Arthur, and as a consequence the word *knight* acquired its considerably more lofty associations.

In the introduction to this section I referred to the tendency for borrowed words to trigger changes in the meanings of existing words in the English lexicon. An example of this can be seen in the history of the word *dream*. This word appears in OE as the word *dream*, meaning 'mirth, music'. As a result of the Viking invasions it came into contact with the ON cognate *draumr* which had the sense 'vision during sleep'. During the early thirteenth century the ME *dreme* started to acquire this new sense, while the OE sense of 'mirth, music' was gradually lost. The sense of 'mirth' is last recorded in the early thirteenth century, while its last use as 'music' was in the early fourteenth century. But this was not a straightforward replacement; there were consequences for the OE word *swefn*, which meant 'vision during sleep', and which became obsolete by the end of the ME period. Similar effects were caused by contact with French, as seen in the fate of the OE word *rīce* which meant 'powerful' or 'mighty'. During the EME period this word began to be used with the sense 'wealthy', the result of contact with the OF word *riche*.

A good example of the complex reshuffling that is necessitated following the adoption of a loanword whose meaning corresponds closely with an existing word can be seen after the introduction of the ON loanword *skȳ*. This word meant 'cloud' in ON and this is the sense in which it is first used when it appears in the written record in the early thirteenth century. By the beginning of the fourteenth century it had begun to be used in its modern sense, creating an overlap with two other words derived from OE: *heven* (OE *heofon*) and *welcen* (OE *wolcen*). While these three words overlapped in the sense of 'sky', they did have subsidiary meanings that allowed them to be disambiguated. While *heven* and *welcen* could both be used to mean 'sky', *heven* was also used to refer to the 'heavens', while *welcen* had the alternative meaning 'cloud'. The picture became even more complex when OE *clūd*, which during the OE period meant 'rock, hill', began to be used as 'cloud' at the beginning of the fourteenth century. This triggered a series of changes, so that *heven* lost the general sense of 'sky' and became a purely religious term to refer to the heavens. The word *sky* ceased to be used to mean 'cloud', while the word *wolcen*, which no longer had a meaning not covered by *cloud*, *heven* or *sky*, fell out of use entirely.

Another cause of semantic change is the existence of a gap in the lexicon of the language. This can be well exemplified by the history of the English colour terms. OE had comparatively few colour terms so that some terms were used with a much wider range of reference than in PDE. The word *red* was used to describe objects like fire, lips, rubies and wine, just as it is today, but, less obviously, it was also used to describe gold. The reasons for this may stem from the lack of a separate word for the colour orange. In the sixteenth century this gap was filled by the use of the noun *orange* as an adjective to describe shades between red and yellow on the colour spectrum. A similar story lies behind the fourteenth-century use of the name of the flower *violet* as a colour adjective indicating a shade in-between blue and purple.

Some words change their meaning via a process known as 'narrowing', or 'specialization', which refers to the shift from a more general meaning to a more specific one. An example of this is the word *meat*, which derives from the OE word *mēat*. In OE this word could refer to any kind of food, whereas its meaning has since narrowed so that it refers to a particular type of food: the flesh of an animal. The opposite process is known as 'widening', where a word's meaning changes from a restricted to a more general application, as in the word *bird*. In OE the general term for the species of birds was *fugol*, while OE *bridd* referred specifically to a 'young bird'. As early as the thirteenth century the ME *brid* had begun to be used as a general term for the species, as in this example from Chaucer: 'No lyues creature, Be it of fissh or bryd or beest or man.' This extension of meaning did not lead to the immediate loss of the more specialized sense of 'young bird', which continued to appear throughout the ME period. It is found in Shakespeare and survives in northern dialect usage. The opposite process can be seen in the fortunes of the OE word *fugol*, although this word retained its generic sense into the seventeenth century. However during the sixteenth century *fowl* began to be used in the specialized sense of domestic cocks and hens, the sense which eventually came to replace its earlier, broader, meaning.

A further cause of meaning change is exaggeration or overstatement, which causes a word's sense to be weakened. This is apparent in the history of the word *soon* which in OE meant 'immediately', as it still does in the phrase *as soon as*, but which now means 'in a short while'. A similar process lies behind a number of words which originally meant 'immediately' and which have been similarly weakened to refer to a time in the near future, e.g. *anon*, *directly*, *presently*.

Another cause of semantic change is the result of euphemistic usage, where the meanings of a number of words are extended to refer to a concept indirectly. Our desire to avoid talking directly about death has led to the formation of numerous euphemisms such as *pass on, pass away, kick the bucket*. It is a frequent feature of euphemisms that they are continually replaced as they begin to acquire the negative connotations of the word they were intended to replace. We can see this in the number of words that have been used for the toilet in English. The word *lavatory* was introduced from Latin *lavatorium* in the fourteenth century to refer to a bath. In the seventeenth century it came to refer to the bathroom and subsequently specifically to the place where one relieves oneself (another euphemism). But once this meaning was widespread another euphemism was required, so that we find the eighteenth-century coinage *water-closet*, or *WC*. Once this had become widespread we find the French loan *toilet* (originally a cloth, extended to refer to a towel used in washing and then a dressing room) being extended in the nineteenth century to take on its modern meaning. In the early twentieth century we get the more common word *loo*, of obscure origin, though possibly derived from *Waterloo* and first attested in Joyce's *Ulysses*. The constant requirement for polite euphemisms lies behind the thirteenth-century borrowing of the French word *privy* (from the adjective *privé* 'private, confidential'). This word survives into modern English but with the more specialized sense of an outdoor toilet. The seventeenth-century adoption of the loanword *latrine* (Latin *latrina* 'private'), now used to refer specifically to a toilet on a military camp or barracks shows a similar process at work.

Another type of semantic change is known as 'pejoration', a term used to describe words which acquire connotations of disapproval that were not present in their original meaning. An example of this is the word *silly* which in OE meant 'happy' and 'blessed', but which in ME developed new meanings such as 'helpless', 'deserving of pity', 'weak', which existed alongside the OE senses. By the fifteenth century the OE senses had died out, with new senses emerging including 'foolish, stupid'. These senses ultimately replaced all of the positive meanings, with 'innocent, helpless and deserving of pity' all dying out in the nineteenth century. There are a number of words that have followed a similar path, such as *crafty*, which meant 'strong, mighty' or 'skilful, dexterous, clever' in OE, although the first sense became obsolete in LME. The negative sense 'wily, cunning' emerged in LME and coexisted with the favourable meaning, finally replacing it in the seventeenth century.

The opposite process, known as 'melioration', occurs when a word acquires positive connotations, as in the ME word *shrewede*. This adjective derives from the noun *shrewe*, 'a wicked or depraved person', and so the adjective meant 'wicked, vicious'. In the sixteenth century it began to be used to mean 'cunning, artful' and from this the more positive sense 'astute, clever' developed. The OE adjective *smeart* originally meant 'sharp, stinging' and was used to describe a whip or a rod, intended to inflict pain. The adjective continued to be use in this sense throughout the ME period and was extended to refer to people with the sense 'bold, arrogant'. The PDE use of *smart* to mean 'witty, clever' began to appear in the seventeenth century, the point when the earlier, negative uses began to die out.

Another important cause of semantic change is metaphorical usage. When we think of metaphor we tend to think specifically of poetic language and extended literary comparisons. But in fact metaphor is a very common feature of everyday language and is so pervasive that we often fail to notice it. Many of the words we use to describe mental processes derive from metaphorical uses of words describing physical activities. For instance, thinking is often associated with visual processes: *he is very switched on; I am in the dark; the lights are on but no one is home.* The meanings of many words have changed to incorporate metaphorical uses that occur from observation of certain similarities with other concepts. For example, the meaning of the word *leaf* was extended due to the recognition of similarities with a piece of paper, so that we now think of 'leaf of a book' as one of its core meanings. The universality of such metaphors is apparent from the way that other languages have undergone similar extensions: thus the Latin word *folio* is from Latin *folium* 'leaf', while the German word *Blatt* means both 'leaf' and 'page'.

Another cause of semantic change is the need to disambiguate words of identical form. One of the results of sound change in the history of English is the creation of homonymic or homophonic clashes: that is, where two or more words have the same spelling or sound or both. Homonymy refers to two words that are identical in spelling and sound, such as in the verb *bear* and the noun *bear*. Homophony refers to words that are identical in sound, but whose spelling differs, as in the noun *bear* and the adjective *bare*. In some cases of homonymy both words have survived but one has been narrowed to avoid confusion. For instance, ME had two identical verbs *leten* with completely contrasting meanings: one meant to allow (as in PDE 'let me have a go') and one meant prevent or obstruct. The result of this clash was the specialization of the second meaning so that it became used only in sporting contexts; if a serve goes in the net in tennis, or a player obstructs a shot in squash, then a *let*, or 'obstruction' is called.

Contact between dialects in ME could also create homonymic or homophonic clashes. For instance, the verb *clippen*, meaning 'cut', was borrowed from ON *klippa* in the East Midland and Northern dialects of ME. During the fourteenth century immigration into London from these dialect areas led to the adoption of this word in the London dialect. However, the word was identical with an existing one meaning 'kiss', from OE *clyppan*. London writers of this period used both words but evidently recognized the potential for confusion, avoiding this by glossing the recent borrowing, as in Chaucer's *clippe or shere*. As this verb became more widely adopted, so the homonym *clippe* meaning 'kiss' became more restricted. It appears in Shakespeare but subsequently fell out of use in the seventeenth century.

Another important example of contact between different dialects as a factor in causing homophonic clashes concerns the diffusion and adoption of the third person plural pronoun *they*, another ON borrowing that is recorded earliest in the East Midlands and Northern dialects and only later in London English. The appearance of this form in London coincided with the loss of the final fricative sound in the word *þeigh* (derived from OE *þēah* 'though') leading to a homophonic clash. To remedy the situation another ON loanword was adopted: *though* (from ON *þó*). This example is of particular interest in suggesting that homophonic clash can trigger change even when the words belong to different word classes: in this case a pronoun and a conjunction.

Despite these examples, the significance of homonymic clash as a motivation for semantic change has been questioned; it is probably best thought of as one of many factors that can influence change. It is perhaps most significant as a factor in cases where the words are of the same grammatical category, phonologically identical, semantically related and used in the same sphere of discourse. There are more homophones than homonyms in PDE, the reason for this being that during the process of standardization of spelling, the spelling of many ME words was remodelled to avoid homonymy. Homophony is of course harder to remove and in spoken discourse homophones are unlikely to cause communicative difficulty.

Now that we have considered the various types of semantic change and attempted to categorize these, I want to end the chapter by considering examples that are harder to classify according to the various criteria I have outlined above. The purpose of this is to emphasize the fact that, while it is possible to generalize about semantic change in the way that I have, individual cases are often considerably more complex and can seldom be attributed to one single factor.

The first example to consider is the noun *deer*, the general name of a family of ruminant quadrupeds, distinguished by the possession of deciduous branching horns or antlers, and by the presence of spots on the young. This word derives from OE *dēor*, used in OE as a generic term for an animal. This change is often simply categorized as an example of narrowing or specialization, similar to the process described above for the word *meat*. A word which originally referred to a wide category became restricted to a small subset of that category. This description is fine as far as it goes, but is ultimately unsatisfactory because it fails to address the more demanding question of why this change should have occurred. When we attempt to answer this question we find that a variety of factors may have played a role. The restriction of *deer* from its general meaning may be due to the introduction of the French loanword *beast* with a similar meaning around 1200. Rather than have two words with similar meanings, speakers began to use *deer* in a more restricted way. But words do not exist in isolation, and the history of *deer* is connected to that of the word *hert*, a ME equivalent to PDE *deer*. If there was already a word meaning 'deer', then why did *deer* take on this meaning rather than refer to some other animal? A possible explanation for this is due to a homonymic clash with OE *heorte* 'heart', which in ME became *herte* and so became identical with ME *hert* 'deer'. This clash led to the restriction of *hert*, not in terms of meaning but in terms of register: *hart* became a technical hunting term. This restriction of *hert* left a gap for a general word for 'deer' which was then filled by the word *deer*. What this example shows is that a variety of different factors may affect the meaning of a word, and that words do not change their meanings in isolation.

My second example concerns the fate of the OE verbs *sweltan* and *steorfan*, both of which meant 'die'. In origin both of these words were probably euphemisms, they derive from Germanic roots that meant 'burn slowly' and 'grow stiff'. In the ME period the ON verb *deyja* was borrowed and, probably due to its close link with the existing noun and adjective (OE *dēaþ*, *dēad*), this verb became adopted as the main verb for 'die'. As a result the two OE verbs became specialized according to their original meanings, so that *swelten* came to mean 'swoon, or faint with heat' (PDE *swelter*) and *steruen* to mean 'die of hunger or cold', which has been further specialized in PDE *starve*. So the reason for this process of narrowing in both verbs was evidently due to the adoption of a loanword with a similar range of reference causing both words to shift their conceptual meanings. But it may be that other processes were at work here as well. The process by which *sterven* became narrowed to refer to 'dying of hunger or cold' was perhaps also influenced by exaggeration or overstatement, just as today the meaning of *starve* is continually weakened so that *I'm starving* means 'I'm really hungry'; those who are genuinely dying of hunger in the third world are usually referred to as 'starving to death'. A similar process may lie behind the restriction of *swelten*, as is also apparent in present-day usage, where *I'm sweltering* just means 'I'm really hot' rather than 'I'm dying of heat exposure'. Here the reason for the change in meaning in the two verbs is clearly pressure from a new loan, while the direction in which they changed was determined by other meanings already available in their variational spaces which were emphasized due to overstatement. A further factor may also be at work in this process. It has also been suggested that these changes were also affected by phonaesthetic factors (Samuels, 1972). In late ME and EModE a number of words with initial /sw/ signified fainting or being too hot, such as *sweal* 'burn, be scorched', *swalm* 'faintness', *swoon*, *sway*, *sweat*, *swime* 'a swoon', *sweam* 'a fainting fit'. Perhaps the existence of these words reinforced the shift in meaning of *swelten* towards 'fainting from heat'. A similar reinforcement process may lie behind the change in meaning of *sterven*, given the appearance of a number of contemporary words with initial /st/ with a similar range of meanings: e.g. *stark, stiff, stern, steeve* 'rigid', *stour* 'severe', *strain* 'afflict', *stress* 'affliction'.

My final example concerns the fate of the OE word *draca*, a Latin loanword which was used in ME to mean 'dragon, battle standard' or 'Satan' (Burnley, 1992). During the ME period the word *dragon* was derived from the accusative form of the same Latin word, *draconem*, via French, and was used with a very similar range of meanings as *drake*. During the thirteenth century another word joined the group: *drake* 'male duck'. While the overlap with *dragon* made *drake* redundant, the appearance of a homonym with a very different meaning also put pressure on this word. The fact that both words were pronounced and spelled identically, belonged to the same word class and were related as hyponyms of the same superordinate term, 'beast', meant that there was a potential for confusion. Imagine how much of an anticlimax it would be for a reader to be following the exploits of a great chivalric hero who has come to the castle to save the beautiful princess who has been held captive by a hideous fire breathing duck? It is of course unlikely that any reader of ME romance would actually confuse the two, but it may be that the potential for such confusion and the ridiculousness of the connotations of *drake* in such contexts was enough to lead to its avoidance in favour of the much more appropriate and threatening *dragon*.

5.10 Further reading

In this chapter we have surveyed the various methods by which the English lexicon has been augmented throughout its history. We have seen that while methods of word formation and borrowing have been active throughout the history of English, their relative importance has varied across the different time periods. Where OE made comparatively little use of borrowing but relied considerably upon word formation, later periods of English show the introduction of loanwords on an impressive scale. But the effects of borrowing go beyond the mere introduction of new words and often lead to the restructuring of other words and meanings in the same semantic field. This kind of restructuring leads to changes in the meanings of words, which are frequently triggered by a complex interaction of factors both linguistic, such as changes in pronunciation leading to homophony, or sociolinguistic, such as contact with other languages and societies.

If you want to read a more comprehensive account of the make up of the lexicon in each of the periods discussed in this chapter, then you should consult the relevant chapters of the first three volumes of the *Cambridge History of the English Language* (Hogg, 1992; Blake, 1992; Lass 1999). For a readable introductory historical study of the English lexicon see Hughes (2000). If you are interested in the theoretical issues treated in this chapter, then a more advanced treatment can be found in Samuels (1972): Chapters 4 and 5. For studies of how literary writers have exploited word formation processes see the studies of Chaucerian and Shakespearean word formation by Horobin (2009) and Nevalainen (2001). Marchand (1969), which takes a diachronic approach to the study of word formation, is the standard work on the subject, though quite advanced for the beginner. For a helpful introduction to PDE morphology and word formation see Jeffries (2006), sections 3.1–3.3, and the introductory work by Adams (1973). Serjeantson (1935/1961) is an exhaustive descriptive survey of borrowing practices throughout the history of English. Jeffries (2006), Chapter 6, provides a useful introduction to the study of semantics and Waldron (1979) gives a lucid overview of the types of semantic change, supplemented by detailed discussions of specific examples.

Morphology   6

OE differs substantially from PDE in that it employed a system of special endings, known as 'inflexions', to mark case, number (singular or plural) and gender (masculine, feminine or neuter). Because the concepts of case and grammatical gender have less formal significance in PDE than they did in OE it is important to begin by explaining them. Case refers to the function of a word within a sentence. OE distinguishes between four major cases: nominative, accusative, genitive and dative. The nominative case describes the subject of the sentence, while the accusative refers to the direct object. So in the sentence 'the boy kicked the ball', *boy* would be in the nominative case as it is the subject and *ball* would be in the accusative case as it is the direct object. The genitive case is used to denote possession, as it is today with the 's and s' ending in PDE. Thus *the boy's book* is a genitive phrase. The dative case is used for the indirect object, so in the sentence 'the boy kicked the ball to the girl', the girl would be in the dative case as she is indirectly affected by the boy's action. The dative case was also commonly used in OE after certain prepositions, although some prepositions were followed by the genitive or accusative cases (especially ones that involve motion). In OE these cases were indicated by the addition of inflexional endings, whereas in PDE we rely on word order to identify the function of a word within a sentence. So in the sentence 'the dog bit the man' we know that *the dog* is the subject and *the man* is the object because of where they appear in the sentence. If we reversed them so that it read 'the man bit the dog', this would change the meaning entirely. Because OE relied more on inflexional endings to carry such information, its word order was more fluid. Languages which make comparatively less use of inflexions, relying instead on word order and prepositions to carry grammatical information, are known as 'analytical' languages. Languages that rely more heavily on inflexional endings to perform these tasks are known as 'synthetic' languages. There are, however, some inflexions in PDE grammar, as we saw above in the inflexional <-s> that is added to nouns to indicate possession, e.g. *boy's* or *boys'*, as well as the -s added to a noun to indicate when it is plural, e.g. *boys*.

Grammatical gender is another problematic category for speakers of PDE as it does not survive into PDE. All nouns in OE belong to one of three genders: masculine, feminine and neuter. The choice of category had nothing to do with sex, or real-world gender, so that the noun *wif*, meaning 'woman', was neuter, while *wifmann*, also meaning 'woman', was masculine. Rather than referring to natural gender, grammatical gender is a way of classifying nouns into certain morphological categories, dependent on the patterns of inflexions that they adopt. These distinctions also affect the words which are linked with a particular noun within a noun phrase. So in the noun phrase 'the good book', the determiner *the* and the adjective *good* must both agree with the noun *book*. Similar systems are found in many modern languages, such as French and German, where different forms of determiners and adjectives are needed depending on the gender of the noun they accompany. The French noun *book* is masculine and so the masculine form of the definite article, *le*, is required: *le livre* 'the book', whereas the noun *table* is feminine and so takes the feminine article: *la table* 'the table'. If we add the adjective *petit* 'little' to the noun phrase then we can see that an inflexional -e is added when it agrees with a feminine noun: *le petit livre, la petite table*. The same principles of agreement within the noun phrase apply in OE, so that determiners and adjectives vary depending on the case, gender and number of the noun that they are accompanying.

So, we have seen that there are major differences between OE and PDE in the way that grammatical information such as case is indicated, and in the replacement of a grammatical gender system with a system of natural gender. In this chapter we will be investigating how and why these major structural changes took place.

6.1 Nouns

We have seen above that OE nouns adopted inflexional endings to indicate case and number, in the following section we will look in detail at the different endings that were used. We have also seen the patterns of inflexions varied according to gender, so that the masculine, feminine and neuter genders must be considered separately. There is a further complication in that there were different categories of nouns within each of the three genders, although here we will focus on the most common type. The first table given here shows the endings that were added to the largest group of masculine nouns in OE. I have used the masculine noun *stān* 'stone' as an example:

Case	Sing.	Plural
Nominative	stān	stānas
Accusative	stān	stānas
Genitive	stānes	stāna
Dative	stāne	stānum

Here we can see the range of different endings that were added to a noun to indicate its function in the sentence. However, if we look closely we will see that not all cases are distinguished in this way. Earlier in this chapter we saw that OE distinguished between the subject and the object by means of inflexions, whereas PDE relies on word order. But in the above table there is no formal distinction between the subject and object cases, the nominative and accusative, in either the singular or plural. The significance of this lack of distinction between these two cases is apparent if we compare it with the equivalent endings found in an older Germanic dialect, Gothic:

Case	Sing.	Plural
Nominative	dags	dagōs
Accusative	dag	dagans
Genitive	dagis	dagē
Dative	daga	dagam

A similar pattern of overlap is also evident in the major category of neuter nouns, which has a similar system of endings to the masculine:

Case	Sing.	Plural
Nominative	scip	scipu
Accusative	scip	scipu
Genitive	scipes	scipa
Dative	scipe	scipum

Apart from the nominative and accusative plural ending in -u, the neuter noun takes the same endings as the masculine noun. Just like the masculine noun, the neuter noun has identical forms in both singular and plural forms of the nominative and accusative. The major feminine noun category shows even more overlap and an even more restricted range of inflexions, with the majority of forms ending in -e or -a.

Case	Sing.	Plural
Nominative	giefu	giefa, -e
Accusative	giefe	giefa, -e
Genitive	giefe	giefa
Dative	giefe	giefum

As with the General masculine noun declension, this paradigm shows considerable reduction of distinctiveness when compared with the equivalent declension in Gothic:

Case	Sing.	Plural
Nominative	giba	gibōs
Accusative	giba	gibōs
Genitive	gibōs	gibō
Dative	gibai	gibōm

There was a further category of nouns in OE, known as the 'weak' declension. This group shows even more evidence of overlap in endings. Here is the declension of the OE weak noun *guma* 'man'.

Case	Sing.	Plural
Nominative	guma	guman
Accusative	guman	guman
Genitive	guman	gumena
Dative	guman	gumum

In this paradigm virtually all non-nominative endings end in -n, apart from the genitive plural in -a and the dative plural in -um. Let us compare this declension with the Gothic equivalent endings for the Gothic noun *guma* 'man':

Case	Sing.	Plural
Nominative	guma	gumans
Accusative	guman	gumans
Genitive	gumins	gumanē
Dative	gumin	gumam

So, while OE did have a variety of inflexional endings, there was already a certain amount of overlap and ambiguity. Some endings were distinctive, such as the -um ending which marks the dative plural, and the -a for the genitive plural; endings which remain consistent across all four of these tables. However -e could be used to mark the dative singular in nouns of all three genders, as well as the accusative and genitive singular, nominative and accusative plural of feminine nouns.

This lack of distinctiveness in the endings led to a certain amount of confusion in the late OE period, but in the EME period things got considerably more complex as a result of major phonological changes. The transition from OE to ME is marked by a process of levelling of unstressed syllables, so that the vowels -u, -a, -e all became pronounced with a schwa, /ə/, the same sound used at the end of the word *china*. As well as this process of levelling of vowel sounds, the nasal consonants /n/ and /m/ were also merged when they appeared in unstressed syllables. The result of this is that the amount of overlap and ambiguity in the system of noun inflexions was considerably increased, leaving just three distinct noun inflexions: -e, -en, -es. Thus one of the principal causes of the move away from a synthetic structure was phonological: as the inflexional endings that carried the grammatical information were eroded, so there became an increasing need for alternative methods of indicating this information.

This reduction in the reliance upon inflexional endings had a knock-on effect on the OE system of grammatical gender, contributing to its complete loss in the EME period. As we saw in the introduction to this chapter, OE had a system whereby nouns were classified into three genders: masculine, feminine and neuter. The loss of inflexions in the OE noun paradigm had a major impact upon the grammatical gender system, with many nouns simply adopting the endings of the dominant class of nouns. But another factor also influenced the fate of the grammatical gender system: that of real-world gender. While there were many examples of nouns where grammatical gender and real-world gender did not correspond, as in the examples of *wif* and *wifmann* cited above, there were also a large number of instances where there was a correspondence, as in the noun *hlafdige*, 'lady', which is feminine (Platzer, 2001). During the late OE and early ME period there was an increasing tendency to indicate the real-world sex of a noun rather than its grammatical gender, particularly in contexts where a pronoun refers back to a noun that is separated from it in the sentence (Jones, 1988). This process began earliest in the north and can be found in late Northumbrian OE texts like the gloss to the *Lindisfarne Gospels* or the *Durham Ritual*. By the end of the thirteenth century the change had affected most dialects of EME, apart from Kentish, which still shows traces of gender into the fourteenth century.

In addition to the obscuration of unstressed syllables and the loss of grammatical gender, the EME period also witnessed the restructuring of the systems of noun inflexions. Where OE had a variety of categories of noun, known as declensions, the majority of nouns transferred to the main masculine declension, represented in the table above by the noun *stān*. The success of this declension over the alternatives was probably due to its more distinctive endings, perhaps reinforced by the fact that it was also the commonest noun type. So what we find in the ME period is the following:

Case	Sing.	Plural
Nominative	ston	stones
Accusative	ston	stones
Genitive	stones	stones, stone
Dative	stone	stones, stonen

But even this reduced set of endings was variable and set to be reduced further. The -e ending in the dative singular became optional and was lost by the late ME period, except after prepositions in certain fossilized phrases like *on honde*. The genitive and dative plural endings -e (from OE -a) and -en (from OE -um) subsequently became replaced by the -es ending, producing a system which differs little from that of PDE.

Alongside this dominant system there remained a much less common type that was derived from the weak declension, which formed its plural in -en. The only relic of this declension that remains in PDE is the noun *ox*, with its plural *oxen*, although the noun *child*, a neuter noun which had the plural *cildru* in OE, has subsequently transferred to this declension. There were more such nouns in ME than there are in PDE, although even in ME they frequently appeared alongside variants with the -es plural, e.g. *toon, toos, shoos, shoon.*

There were few further changes to the inflexion system in the EModE period, although several innovations affected the genitive case. At the end of the ME period the genitive singular and plural were identical, both took the ending -(e)s and so an attempt was made to disambiguate using punctuation. The apostrophe 's was introduced in the singular form in the second half of the seventeenth century while the s' form was adopted for the plural in the eighteenth century. Another method of marking the genitive emerged in the sixteenth and seventeenth centuries, the so-called *his*-genitive. This is the use of the possessive pronoun *his* instead of the -es noun inflexion, so that we find constructions such as the *man his book* rather than *the manis book.* The reason for this may be that speakers mistakenly understood the /ɪz/ inflexion to be a reduced form of the pronoun *his* and so restored it. This genitive form is particularly associated with nouns ending in sibilant consonants (i.e. /s, z, ʃ, ʒ/). An alternative explanation for the emergence of this construction is that it was deletion of the initial [h] in *his* that led to homophony with the genitive inflexion, causing the two forms to be associated with each other in speakers' minds. It is interesting that this construction was also extended to feminine nouns, so that in the papers of the Cely family we find 'Margaret ys doghter', literally 'Margaret his daughter'. A logical development of this was the use of the feminine possessive pronoun *hir* in this position, and then the use of the plural pronoun *their* for plurals. But this innovation did not last; the success of the apostrophe led to its obsolescence in the late seventeenth century. Other alternative genitive constructions were the endingless or 'zero genitive', particularly associated with names ending in -s, and the periphrastic constructions using *of,* as we find today in Lloyds Bank (with no apostrophe) and the Bank of England. The periphrastic construction was particularly associated with non-personal nouns, while personal nouns tended to form their genitive using the -(e)s inflexion.

There was little change in the noun plural endings during EModE, although -n plurals became increasingly less common. Some of the ME examples continue to appear, e.g. *eyne* 'eyes', while some new unhistorical -n plurals were formed, e.g. *brethren* and *children.* Such forms were often used purely as a metrical convenience, as shown by a comparison of the following examples from Shakespeare:

> And thence from Athens turn away our eyes,
> To seek new friends and stranger companies.
> *(Midsummer Night's Dream* 1.1.218–9)

> O Helen, goddess, nymph, perfect, divine!
> To what, my love, shall I compare thine eyne?

> (*Midsummer Night's Dream* 3.2.137–8)

Plurals formed using the -n inflexion were condemned by eighteenth-century grammarians who considered them to be provincial and advised against their use.

6.2 Determiners

In this section we will consider the development of the determiner system: which includes the definite and indefinite articles and the demonstratives, *this, these, that, those*. OE differed quite markedly from PDE in its use of determiners: there is, for instance, no indefinite article like PDE *a(n)*: its ancestor, OE *ān*, was a numeral meaning 'one', although *sum* 'a certain' could be used in a similar way to the PDE indefinite article . Another difference is that the OE definite article, equivalent to PDE *the*, could also function as a demonstrative with the meaning 'that'. The beginnings of the PDE system can be traced during the ME period, when we see the formation of a system with distinct sets of indefinite and definite articles and demonstratives. The indefinite article emerged in the EME period, when it was inflected for case, although this inflection is later lost to give a system like that of PDE where <a> is the main form with <an> appearing before vowels.

The origins of the PDE form of the definite article are rather mysterious, in that none of the various forms of the OE determiner system is an obvious ancestor. As we saw in the previous section, the determiner had to agree with the noun in number, case and gender. As a consequence there were different forms of the determiner for each of the three genders and for each of the four cases, although the plural did not distinguish between masculine, feminine and neuter. The various forms are set out in the following table:

Sing.	Masc.	Fem.	Neut.	Plural
Nominative	se	sēo	þæt	þā
Accusative	þone	þā	þæt	þā
Genitive	þæs	þǣre	þæs	þāra, þǣra
Dative	þǣm	þǣre	þǣm	þǣm, þām

Despite the variety of different forms recorded for the OE determiner, not one is similar to our PDE definite article *the*; the most likely explanation for its origin is that it derives from the masculine nominative singular form, *se*, with the *þ*- being adopted by analogy with the other forms in the paradigm. This development appears earliest in the Mercian and Northumbrian dialects of OE and is widespread throughout early ME, so that by the middle of the thirteenth century *se* had disappeared completely, apart from the Kentish dialect where *ze* (masc) and *zy* (feminine) survived into the fourteenth century.

During the EME period the determiner continued to be inflected to indicate case distinctions, although these distinctions were quickly lost in favour of a system where there is just one singular form: *þe* and one plural form: *þo*, derived from the nominative and accusative plural *þā*. By the fourteenth century the plural form *þo* became less common and was subsequently replaced by the singular form, producing the modern usage where there is just one form, *the*, for both singular and plural. While the loss of inflected forms representing case and grammatical gender is expected given the changes occurring elsewhere in the grammatical system, the loss of a distinct plural form is less easily explained. As we saw when we looked at the noun declensions, the singular/plural distinction is one of the few distinctions that has been preserved throughout the history of English. The loss of this distinction is difficult to explain, especially given its survival in other determiners, like *this/these* and *that/those* as we shall see below.

OE had another demonstrative, *þes* 'this', found also in ON but not in Gothic. As with the determiner, the paradigm shows different forms for the three genders in the singular but the same form for all in the plural:

Case	Masc.	Fem.	Neut.	Plural
Nominative	þes	þēos	þis	þās
Accusative	þisne	þās	þis	þās
Genitive	þis(s)es	þisse	þis(s)es	þissa
Dative	þis(s)um	þisse	þis(s)um	þis(s)um

The *þes* 'this' paradigm decayed in a similar way to that of *se*, with *þis* becoming generalized as the singular form in the ME period. A new plural form *þise* was formed, with the -e probably being adopted from the adjective plural, though metrical evidence suggests that the final -e was not pronounced; this form was replaced in the fifteenth century by *þese*, the ancestor of PDE *these*. In the thirteenth century the OE nominative and accusative neuter determiner *þat* took on a new role as a distal demonstrative, indicating an object in the distance, with the sense of 'that' rather than 'the'. This new role was encouraged by the loss of grammatical gender, which meant that there was no longer any need for a separate neuter determiner. The earliest instances of this development are found in the *Ormulum* where we find *þatt* being used with all nouns, irrespective of their grammatical gender, with the sense 'that' rather than 'the'.

In EME *þo* is adopted as a plural for *þat*, and then later in the ME period the form *þos* emerged. This form probably arose through the addition of an -s, via analogy with the noun plural, to the singular form *þo*. A similar kind of development lies behind the non-standard plural form of the second person pronoun, *yous*, as described later on in this chapter. The form *þos*, which is the ancestor of our PDE standard form *those*, does not appear in the southern dialects of ME until the fifteenth century; Chaucer's usage is the older paradigm of *that/tho*. Interestingly this standard form has not been widely adopted in dialect usage, and present-day dialects use a number of variant forms, such as 'look at them flowers', or 'them there flowers', or 'yon flowers' or less commonly 'look at they flowers'.

6.3 Adjectives

In the previous sections we noted that OE employed a system of agreement within the noun phrase so that determiners and nouns agreed in number, gender and case. This same process of agreement applied to adjectives as well, with the result that adjectives took different endings depending upon the noun they were modifying. A further complication is that a different set of endings was used depending on whether the adjective was 'weak' (or indefinite) or 'strong' (or definite). Weak adjectives are ones that are preceded by a determiner, whereas a strong adjective is one that stands on its own. The two sets of endings are as follows:

Weak paradigm

Sing.	Masc.	Fem.	Neut.	Plural
Nominative	gōda	gōde	gōde	gōdan
Accusative	gōdan	gōdan	gōde	gōdan
Genitive	gōdan	gōdan	gōdan	gōdra/gōdena
Dative	gōdan	gōdan	gōdan	gōdum

Strong paradigm

Sing.	Masc.	Fem.	Neut.	Plural
Nominative	gōd	gōd	gōd	gıde
Accusative	gōdne	gōde	gōd	gıd
Genitive	gōdes	gōdre	gōdes	gōdra
Dative	gōdum	gōdre	gōdum	gōdum

The process of inflexional simplification and loss that we noted above in the noun and determiner paradigms had similar effects on the adjectives. The only inflexional category that survived the ME period was number, with plural adjectives taking an -e ending. In addition to the reduction in the markers of case, the strong/weak opposition also decayed. It survived longest in monosyllabic adjectives ending in a consonant, such as *good, old, yong*, which added an -e ending when following a determiner. So the ME equivalent of the above paradigms is the following:

	Weak	Strong
Singular	goode	good
Plural	goode	goode

This system is still found in the works of LME poets like Chaucer and Hoccleve, as in the following line from Chaucer: 'And whan this goode man saugh that it was so', where the adjective *good* takes an -e inflexion because it follows the determiner *this*. By the late fourteenth century the weak adjective inflexion was probably a poetic device rather than a living feature of the language; fifteenth-century scribes show little understanding of the principles governing the weak/strong distinction and frequently add or omit final -e at random.

A further development in the LME period was the appearance of an -s plural adjective ending, whose appearance can be linked to the similar French practice. This inflexion is mostly restricted to romance adjectives which appear after the noun, another feature of French adjectives, as in Chaucer's *weyes espirituels*.

6.4 Verbs

The OE verb conjugation employed inflexions to mark two tenses: present and preterite, used to distinguish between present and past time. OE verbs also used inflexions to distinguish three moods: indicative, imperative and subjunctive. 'Mood' is an expression of a speaker's attitude to a statement: the indicative mood indicates where a speaker is expressing a fact, whereas the subjunctive mood is used to express uncertainty or possibility. PDE no longer has different forms of the verb to indicate the subjunctive mood and relies on auxiliary verbs such as may, might to indicate hypothetical statements. There is a vestige of the subjunctive form of the verb to be used in conditional statements such as 'If I were you', although most speakers tend to use the indicative in such constructions: 'If I was you.' The imperative mood is used to express commands; in PDE there is just one imperative form, whereas it had both singular and plural form depending on the number of people being addressed. The OE verb also has different inflexions to indicate three persons (1st, 2nd and 3rd person), in both singular and plural. Here are the verb endings for the verb *singan* 'sing':

	Present indicative	Preterite indicative
Singular		
1st	singe	sang
2nd	singest	sunge
3rd	singeþ	sang
Plural		
1st	singaþ	sungon
2nd	singaþ	sungon
3rd	singaþ	sungon

	Present subjunctive	Preterite subjunctive
Singular		
1st	singe	sunge
2nd	singe	sunge
3rd	singe	sunge
Plural		
1st	singen	sungen
2nd	singen	sungen
3rd	singen	sungen

The most striking feature of the above paradigms is the large degree of overlap in the various endings. Although I have distinguished between first, second and third persons in the plural there are in fact no formal distinctions in any of the above conjugations. In the subjunctive there is no distinction between first, second and third persons in the singular either. Furthermore, there is no difference in the endings used for the present and preterite subjunctive forms: both take -e in the singular and -en in the plural. While the present indicative has different endings for the three persons in the singular, there is no distinction between first and third persons singular in the preterite indicative. The above paradigms are those that apply to 'strong' verbs: a group of verbs which formed their past tense by changing the vowel of their stem: *singe-sange*. There was another class of verbs in OE, known as 'weak' verbs, which formed their past tense by adding a dental suffix: an ending containing one of the following inflexions [ɪd d t]. The distinction between strong and weak verbs is still found in PDE, cf. *sing-sang* and *walk-walked*, although there were more strong verbs in OE than there are in PDE. The weak verbs had a different system of endings, as may be exemplified by the following conjugation of the verb *fremman* 'do, perform':

	Present indicative	Preterite indicative
Singular		
1st	fremme	fremede
2nd	fremest	fremedest
3rd	fremeþ	fremede
Plural		
1st	fremmaþ	fremedon
2nd	fremmaþ	fremedon
3rd	fremmaþ	fremedon

As with the strong verb conjugations there is considerable overlap between the various categories: person is only marked in the indicative singular, there is no distinction between present and preterite subjunctive and so on. What these paradigms indicate is that there was considerable simplification in the OE system, with most distinctions being marked by a small number of endings.

	Present subjunctive	Preterite subjunctive
Singular		
1st	fremme	fremede
2nd	fremme	fremede
3rd	fremme	fremede
Plural		
1st	fremmen	fremeden
2nd	fremmen	fremeden
3rd	fremmen	fremeden

The levelling of unstressed syllables that led to the complete restructuring of the noun declensions had similarly major repercussions in the verb conjugations. The reduction of vowels in unstressed syllables to schwa, /ə/, meant that the preterite plural indicative ending -on became -en, making it identical to both the present and past plural subjunctive. The result of this was to remove any formal distinction between the subjunctive and indicative moods. Where OE had distinct endings for the third person singular present and plural indicative forms, -eþ and -aþ, this distinction was lost in ME, with both being spelled -eþ. What emerged was a system with a complete loss of the indicative and subjunctive distinction, a preservation of the present/past distinction and distinctive forms of the second and third person singular present indicative. Here is the present indicative verb conjugation for the ME verb *singen*:

		ME
Singular	1st	singe
	2nd	singest
	3rd	singeth
Plural		singeth

A number of further changes affected this conjugation during the ME period. Although the above conjugation remained stable in the southern dialects throughout the entire period, a different set of endings is found in the northern dialects from the EME period. In the northern dialects an alternative ending, -s, is found for the second and third person singular and plural forms.

These forms gradually percolated south during the ME period and are found in London English of the fifteenth century. An alternative ending for the present plural, -en, was found in the Midlands dialects and this was adopted in London during the fourteenth century following immigration into the capital from the Midlands as described in Chapter 3. Throughout the fourteenth and fifteenth centuries the final <-n> was subject to deletion and was finally lost, so that London English of the late ME period had two rival paradigms:

				PDE
Singular	1st	loue	loue	love
	2nd	louest	louest	love
	3rd	loueth	loues	loves
Plural		loue(n)	loues	love

The first of these paradigms derives from the southern dialects, with the replacement of the OE derived -eth present plural ending with the Midland ending in -e(n). The second paradigm is the northern version, which came into contact with the southern one as a result of immigration from the north Midlands in the fifteenth century.

During the EModE period the interaction between the two systems led to a further series of changes by which the northern -s ending replaced the -eth ending in the third person singular, while the second person singular and plural endings were lost altogether. The result of this is the PDE system, in which there is only one inflexional ending in the present indicative:

	Singular	Plural
1st	sing	sing
2nd	sing	sing
3rd	sings	sing

The process by which the -eth gave way to the -s ending was gradual and the -eth ending was used throughout much of the EModE period. Shakespeare used both forms, although there are more instances of the -s endings in his plays written after 1600. The Authorized Version of the Bible, published in 1611, used the -eth throughout, although its language is often traditional, even archaic. The continued use of the -eth ending in such contexts meant that it became particularly associated with liturgical use. Comments by seventeenth-century grammarians indicate that, where the -eth ending did continue to appear, it was pronounced identically with the -s ending. In *Remaines of a Greater Worke* (1605) William Camden set out to explain Sir Thomas Smith's spelling reforms. In describing Smith's use of the letter <z> Camden wrote that 'he would have vsed [z] for the softer S, or eth, and es, as *diz* for dieth, *liz* for lies'. This explanation shows that, for Camden at least, the <-eth> and <-es> inflexions may be used interchangeably to represent /z/. Camden's evidence is supported by Richard Hodges who, in his *Special Help to Orthography* (1643), explained that, despite its retention in the written language, the -eth form had come to be pronounced as the -es form:

> Howsoever wee use to write thus, *leadeth* it, *maketh* it ... Yet in our ordinary speech ... wee say, *leads* it, *makes* it ... Therefore, whensoever *eth*, cometh in the end of any word, wee may pronounce it sometimes as *s* & sometimes like *z*.

So the evidence indicates that the -s ending began as a northern dialect form which was subsequently adopted as an informal or colloquial alternative to the -eth ending. By the sixteenth century the -s ending was the usual form with -eth being reserved for liturgical and other formal written registers. By the seventeenth century the distinction had become a purely written one paving the way for the complete loss of -eth by around 1750.

6.5 Adverbs

Adverbs were a comparatively straightforward category in OE as they were invariant. They were typically formed by adding -e to the adjective, so *heard* (adjective), *hearde* (adverb). Where the adjective already ended in -e the two were identical, as in *clǣne* (adjective), *clǣne* (adverb). Many OE adjectives end in -lic and this resulted in a number of adverbs ending -lice, such as *cyneli* (adjective), *cynelice* (adverb). This led to a reinterpretation of the adverb ending as -lice, with the result that a number of adverbs appear in OE with both endings, e.g. *fæste/fæstlice*. Doublets of this kind continue to appear in ME with both the -e and -ly inflexion (the ME equivalent of -lice), e.g. *loude/loudly, softe/softly*.

6.6 Pronouns

The personal pronoun is the only word class that has maintained inflexion for number, case and gender throughout the history of English, though there has been considerable simplification to the system found in OE. The OE personal pronoun system had three numbers: singular, dual and plural and four cases: nominative, accusative, genitive and dative. However, the only pronoun to show inflexion for gender was the third person singular; the third person plural forms were the same across all three genders. OE also had a dual pronoun, used to refer to two persons; the following table shows the forms of the dual pronoun as it is found in OE:

	Singular	Plural
Nominative	wit	git
Accusative	unc	inc
Genitive	uncer	incer
Dative	unc	inc

Compared to older Germanic languages such as Gothic, where the dual was marked formally both in the pronoun system and in the verb conjugation, the OE dual was comparatively reduced. Despite this, the dual pronoun survived into early ME, although the earliest ME evidence shows that it was already in decay. So in the *Owl and the Nightingale* we find *wit* for 'we two' appearing alongside *we*.

The next table shows the forms found in OE for the first and second person pronouns:

Old English

Nominative	ic	wē
Accusative	mē, mēc	ūs, ūsic
Genitive	mīn	ūre
Dative	mē	ūs
Nominative	þū	gē
Accusative	þē, þēc	ēow, ēowic
Genitive	þīn	ēower
Dative	þē	ēow

Present-day English

Nominative	I	we
Accusative	me	us
Genitive	mine	our
Nominative	you	you
Accusative	you	you
Genitive	your	your

Compared to older Germanic languages, the OE pronoun system already showed a degree of simplification in the way that the dative and accusative cases had merged: accusative mē, dative mē; accusative þē, dative þē; accusative ūs dative ūs; accusative ēow, dative ēow (although some verse texts and early Anglian texts preserve an older system with distinct 1st/2nd person accusative pronouns: þēc, mēc, ūsic, ēowic). This process of merging, or 'sycretism', continued in the ME period, with the dative forms ousting the accusative forms just as in OE.

The same process also affected the third person pronoun, although things are slightly more complicated here and so we will consider the different forms of this pronoun separately. The following table sets out the various forms of the third person pronoun in OE.

	Singular			Plural
Nominative	hē	hēo	hit	hīe
Accusative	hine	hīe, hī	hit	hīe
Genitive	his	hire	his	hīera
Dative	him	hire	him	him

If we begin by considering the masculine pronoun we can see how the OE system became the PDE one. For while a separate accusative pronoun was preserved throughout the OE period, in the ME period we see it being replaced by the dative pronoun *him*, giving our PDE system. The form *hine* disappeared at different times during the ME period; it was retained in areas of the south and the south-west up until the fourteenth century. In fact a reflex of *hine*, /ən/ still survives in the dialects of south-west England, showing that this form must have been used quite widely in speech throughout the ME period. The feminine accusative singular forms *hī, hie* began to be replaced by the dative *hiere, hire* in the tenth century, though they survived in the south until the late thirteenth century, when they were replaced by *hir(e)/her(e)*. In neuters the acc/dat distinction was maintained throughout most of ME period, and only later *him* was dropped for indirect objects in standard usage (and is still found in the south west).

The OE first person pronoun *Ic* became *Ich* in ME and was replaced by *I* during Chaucer's time. *Ich* survived longer in the more conservative dialects of the south, which accounts for its appearance in Chaucer's works, where it is much less common than the dominant form *I*. In the EModE period it continued to appear as a marked dialect form, as is shown by its use in *King Lear*, where it forms part of the dialect adopted by Edgar in his peasant disguise in the phrase *chill*, i.e. *ich will*: 'Chill pick your teeth, zir.'. The action at this point in the play is set in Dover, which may indicate that this feature was considered Kentish at this time, although it may simply be that *ich* was considered to belong to a generalized rustic dialect.

Perhaps the most obvious difference between the OE paradigm for these pronouns and that of PDE is the presence in OE of a distinct second person singular pronoun. In PDE there is just one pronoun, *you*, which is used for both singular and plural reference. In OE there were distinct singular and plural pronouns, although the sociolinguistic distinction that is found in many modern languages, such as French, where the plural form can be used to address a singular person was not found in OE. What happened to the singular form? Why was this form lost, leaving such an obvious gap in the English pronoun system?

To explain this we need to go back to ME. The ME second person pronoun paradigm is as follows:

Nominative	thou	ye
Accusative	thee	you
Genitive	thyn	your
Dative	thee	you

Apart from a few minor spelling changes and the complete loss of a distinct accusative form, this paradigm is identical with that of OE. However there is a major pragmatic difference in the ways that the singular and plural pronouns were used in ME that cannot be discerned from a simple paradigm. To understand this change we need to look at evidence of ME in use. To exemplify the ways that ME differs from OE we will look at some instances of second person pronoun use in Chaucer's works.

In Chaucer's works it is conventional for courtly men and women to address each other using the plural pronoun, even when it is just one person that is being addressed. So, for example, throughout their lengthy courtship and relationship Troilus and Criseyde consistently use the plural pronoun to address each other. Why should this be? The reason seems to be the result of contact with French during the ME period and the prestige attached to French culture and manners. French maintains what modern sociolinguists call a 'T/V system', where the V pronoun encodes power or status and the T pronoun encodes intimacy or solidarity (Brown & Gilman, 1960). The plural pronoun, *vous*, is used to indicate respect and formality, while the singular form, *tu*, is intended to signal familiarity or a lack of respect. A similar distinction is found in Chaucer's use of *thou* and *ye*, and an understanding of this distinction is important in appreciating the subtleties in the shifting relations between characters in Chaucer's works. The importance of this distinction is apparent from its use in contexts where the power in the relationship is extremely one-sided. For instance, when the marquis Walter sets out the terms of the agreement by which he is willing to marry the humble Griselda in an extremely unromantic marriage proposal, he addresses her using the polite form:

> "I seye this: be ye redy with good herte
> To al my lust, and that I frely may,
> As me best thynketh, do yow laughe or <u>smerte</u>,   suffer
> And nevere ye to <u>grucche</u> it, nyght ne day?   complain
> And <u>eek</u> when I sey 'ye,' ne sey nat 'nay,'   also
> Neither by word ne frownyng <u>contenance</u>?   expression
> Swere this, and heere I swere oure alliance."

(E 351–7)

The singular form, *thou*, is used by socially superior people when addressing those lower down the social scale, or by members of the older generation to younger people. As an example we may compare Walter's use of the polite form in addressing Griselda above, with his use of the singular form to address her father Janicula, whose social inferiority is clearly marked:

> "Janicula, I neither may ne kan
> Lenger the plesance of myn herte hyde.
> If that thou <u>vouche sauf</u>, what so bityde,   promise
> Thy doghter wol I take, <u>er</u> that I wende,   before
> As for my wyf, unto hir lyves ende."

(E 304–8)

As well as expressing social superiority, the use of the singular form can also be used to express disrespect or contempt, as in the Host's deliberately brusque interruption of Chaucer's Tale of Sir Thopas:

> "Namoore of this, for Goddes dignitee,"
> Quod oure Hooste, "for thou makest me
> So wery of thy verray <u>lewednesse</u>" ignorance
>
> (B2 2109–10)

In some instances it is not always possible to decide precisely why a particular form is being used, as in the Franklin's use of the singular form in addressing the Squire when praising his efforts: "In feith, Squier, thow hast thee wel yquit/And gentilly. I preise wel thy wit ... considerynge thy yowthe" (F 673–5). Here the Franklin emphasizes the Squire's youth and the use of the singular pronoun is presumably a means of flagging the age gap, although there is also a suggestion here that the Franklin is deliberately patronizing the Squire.

The singular form may also be used to express familiarity and intimacy. Earlier we noted that Troilus uses the polite form when addressing Criseyde throughout the entire poem. There is, however, a single exception: he switches to the singular form on just one occasion, when pledging his commitment to his lady: 'For I am thyn, by God and by my trouthe!' (3.1512). The same is true of Criseyde, who uses the plural pronoun consistently but switches to the singular form at a moment of similarly high emotional intensity: 'Syn I am thyn al hol, withouten mo' (4.1641). These courtly conventions of formal address are deliberately undermined by Nicholas in the Miller's Tale, whose decidedly uncourtly advances on Alison are marked by the use of the singular pronoun: 'For deerne love of thee, lemman, I spille' (A 3278). Alison's outraged response, although it lasts only a few lines, includes the formal pronoun as part of her attempt to maintain decorum and distance in their relationship. Absolon, who is trying to play the role of the courtly lover, addresses Alison with the plural form, though she always responds with the singular form, indicating her contempt for his advances. Like Troilus, Absolon switches to the singular form at the crucial moment of intimacy, as he prepares to receive a kiss from his lady: 'Lemman, thy grace, and sweete bryd, thyn oore!' (A 3726), while his use of the singular form the next time he addresses her is full of contempt: 'I shal thee quyte.' Switching from *ye* to *thou* as an expression of disrespect and contempt is also found in the Second Nun's Tale, where Cecilia begins by addressing Almachius with the more respectful pronoun, despite the scornful way in which he addresses her and assures him that she is of noble birth:

> "What maner womman artow?" tho quod he.
> "I am a gentil womman born," quod she.

> "I axe thee," quod he, "though it thee greeve,
> Of thy religioun and of thy <u>bileeve</u>."   faith
> "Ye han bigonne youre questioun folily,"
> Quod she, "that wolden two answeres conclude
> In o demande; ye axede <u>lewedly</u>."   ignorantly
>
> (G 424–30)

Having defended herself in an outspoken and unapologetic fashion, she then proceeds to mock Almachius and his demand that she worship his gods and renounce her faith, switching to the singular pronoun to signal the increased contempt and scorn:

> "O juge, confus in thy <u>nycetee</u>,   foolishness
> Woltow that I <u>reneye</u> innocence,   renounce
> To make me a wikked <u>wight</u>?" quod shee.   creature
>
> (G 463–5)

An implication of this usage was that the plural pronoun was frequently used as the default pronoun when referring to a single person. *Thou* was still used to express intimacy or contempt, although this usage became increasingly less common, perhaps in an attempt to avoid over-familiarity or rudeness. The result of this was that *you* became increasingly perceived as the default pronoun, and *thou* became correspondingly rarer.

This sociolinguistic distinction did, however, survive into EModE, where it can be found in Shakespeare's language. A passage in *Twelfth Night* shows clearly how the use of *thou* is considered to be the equivalent of an insult when Sir Toby Belch advises Sir Andrew Aguecheek to use that pronoun as part of a written challenge:

> Go, write it in a martial hand; be curst and briefe; it is no matter how witty, so it be eloquent and full of invention. Taunt him with the license of ink; if thou thou'st him some thrice, it shall not be amiss; and as many lies, as will lie in thy sheet of paper, although the sheet were bigge enough for the bed of Ware in England, set 'em down; go about it. Let there be gall enough in thy ink, though thou write with a goose-pen, no matter. About it.
>
> (*Twelfth Night*, 3.2.39–47)

As we saw in Chapter 2, the EModE period provides evidence from a wider range of non-literary usage than the ME period, and this allows us to identify whether such distinctions continued to be observed in real life. The importance of this T/V distinction is confirmed by a parallel example t that quoted above, from the trial of Sir Walter Raleigh in 1603. In the following quotation Sir Edward Coke, the Attorney General, uses the *thou* form to insult Raleigh:

> All that he did was by thy Instigation, thou Viper; for I thou thee, thou Traitor.

In EModE letters, also closer to actual usage than literary texts, *thou* is found mostly when a parent addresses a child, or between spouses, though even in these situations there is considerable variation, with writers frequently alternating between the two forms. This is well exemplified by the following extract from an early seventeenth-century letter from Katherine Paston to her son (*c.*1624), where the writer switches from the singular pronoun in the opening blessing to the plural pronoun for the more informational part of the letter:

> My good Child the Lord blese the ever more in all thy goinges ovtt and thy Cominges in. euen in all thy ways works and words, for his mercy sake: I was very glad to heer by your first letter that you wer so saffly arriued at your wished portt. (Nevalainen 2006)

The evidence of EModE grammarians shows that the *thou* pronoun continued to be employed as well as providing interesting insights into its connotations. John Wallis (1653) notes that the singular usually implies disrespect or familiarity, while Cooper (1685) identifies *you* as the default pronoun, noting that *thou* is used 'emphaticè, fastidiosè, vel blandè': emphatically, contemptuously or caressingly. While both singular and plural pronouns remained available in the EModE period, it is apparent that the distinction became a purely sociolinguistic one and that the earlier number distinction was no longer salient. The ultimate result of this development was the complete loss of the *thou* pronoun, as is shown by Robert Lowth's Grammar of 1762, which notes that *thou* is obsolete, even when expressing familiarity.

One further, more minor, change was to affect the second person pronoun: the replacement of the subject pronoun *ye* by the object pronoun *you*. This development occurred in the sixteenth century, appearing first in informal contexts and then spreading to more formal ones. Its avoidance in formal prose is apparent from the usage of the Authorized Version of the Bible (1611), which retains the traditional form *ye* throughout:

> But of the fruit of the tree which is in the midst of the garden, God hath said, Ye shall not eat of it, neither shall ye touch it, lest ye die.
>
> (Genesis 3:3)

By the eighteenth century *you* had become the standard singular and plural form for both the nominative and oblique cases, with *ye* and *thou* relegated to special registers, especially religious ones.

The pronoun *thou* continues to survive in religious usage in PDE, as in the Lord's Prayer: 'Hallowed by thy name, thy kingdom come, thy will be done.' It is also used in some northern dialects and in parts of the south-west. Dialect usage also provides evidence of various solutions designed to remedy the lack of a singular/plural distinction. The plural form *yous* is common in Scots and many US dialects, while the form *y'all* is prevalent in southern US dialects.

Now that we have covered the first and second person pronouns it is time to turn to the more complex issues surrounding the development of the third person pronouns, where we have different forms for the masculine, feminine and neuter genders:

	Singular			**Plural**
Nominative	hē	hēo	hit	hīe
Accusative	hine	hīe	hit	hīe
Genitive	his	hire	his	hīera
Dative	him	hire	him	him

For ease of reference I have given the PDE equivalent forms below:

	Singular			**Plural**
Nominative	he	she	it	they
Accusative	him	her	it	them
Genitive	his	her	its	their

There are a number of crucial differences between these two different systems. But we will begin our discussion with the greatest puzzle of all: the development of the third person singular feminine pronoun. The OE forms for the nominative pronoun are *heo* and *hio*, while the form *hie*, which is historically the accusative form, is also sometimes found in nominative position. As none of these forms begins with the sound [ʃ] it is difficult to trace the origins of the modern form. Given that none of the personal pronouns appears to be the origin of the *she* pronoun, scholars have turned to other pronominal forms for evidence of its origin. Some scholars have suggested that the modern form descends from the OE determiner *seo/sio*, although this theory is not especially persuasive as the OE determiner became obsolete early in the ME period, before the emergence of the *she* pronoun. If the origins of *she* cannot be traced in OE then perhaps it has been borrowed from another language, such as Old Norse? The borrowing of closed class words like pronouns is unusual although there are precedents during this period, as we shall see in our discussion of the third person plural pronoun below. But the equivalent pronoun in ON is *hon*, which cannot be the origin of *she*. So where did *she* come from and why was it adopted?

The first point to make is that a problem arose concerning the third person singular pronouns in the late OE period. During the late OE period a sound change occurred whereby OE diphthongs became monophthongs. As a result the diphthong *ēo* in the feminine pronoun *hēo* became *ē*. Thus the feminine pronoun changed from *hēo* to *hē*. This created a problem as it meant that there was no longer any formal difference between the masculine and feminine pronouns. A number of modern languages do not have formally distinct masculine and feminine pronouns (such as Finnish), though it evidently caused communicative problems as can be seen in some early ME texts. So, a sound change led to a systemic gap, whereby two formally distinct pronouns fell together, creating a need for a distinct feminine pronoun. This gap was subsequently filled by *she*, our PDE form. This seems to explain the reason for the change, but it still leaves unsolved the origin of the form that was adopted to remedy the problem. To explain this we need to look at the variety of forms used for the feminine pronoun in EME. The *she* pronoun first appeared in the *Peterborough Chronicle* in the early twelfth century, but it would be wrong to imagine that its ultimate adoption was assured from that moment. While it does appear as the usual form in London English of the late fourteenth century, as witnessed by Chaucer's usage, earlier London texts have spellings beginning with <ȝ> or <ȝh>. Furthermore, contemporary western texts continue to have forms with initial <h>. The north-western poet who wrote *Sir Gawain and the Green Knight* used the form *ho*, clearly descending from OE *hēo*, although there are a handful of examples of *scho* in his works. So, how are we to explain this confusing degree of variation?

Despite there being several hundred different forms of *she* recorded in the dialects of late ME, we can classify all of these into three major types:

1. Type 1 develops from OE *hēo* to give forms beginning with initial <h>.
2. Type 2 has spellings showing initial <ȝ>, <y>, <g>.
3. Type 3 forms begin with <sh>, <sch>.

The origin of the Type 1 forms is straightforward as they clearly derive from the OE forms. The Type 2 spellings are thought to reflect the sounds [hj-], [ç-] or [j-], also derived from OE *heo*, but formed as a result of a process of stress-shifting, or 'resyllabification' of the diphthong, thus either [hjo:] or, following a subsequent assimilatory development, [ço:] or [jo:]. The Type 3 forms clearly indicate a pronunciation with initial [ʃ] and are evidently the origin of the PDE form *she*. The fact that this type is first attested in the *Peterborough Chronicle*, a text produced in an area of dense Norse settlement, suggests that influence from ON played a part in its development, although, as we have seen, ON cannot be the ultimate origin of the form.

The most persuasive explanation that has been offered is that the Type 3 forms derive from the Type 2 forms, via a sound change whereby [hj-]>[ç-]>[ʃ-]. Support for this argument comes from a similar shift in the pronunciation of certain place names in Scotland, such as *Shetland*, which derives from ON *Hjaltland*, and in northern England, like the Cumbrian *Shap*, which was ME *Yhep* (OE *heap* 'pile of stones'). But while these examples do lend support to the hypothesized change from [hj-]>[ç-]>[ʃ-], they are rather limited in number and range. Are a handful of place names sufficient corroborative evidence for a similar change in a high-frequency grammatical item? The lack of other examples for this change can, however, be accounted for. One reason is that the [hj-] or [ç-] sound that is necessary for this development is very rare in accents of English before the modern period, while in the modern period they are rare in non-standard accents. In PDE there are few common words with initial [hj-] or [ç-] so that there is not much opportunity for the change to occur, examples are *huge, human, humid, humiliate*. Where they do appear in standardized accents, a shift to [ʃ] is inhibited by the influence of the standard written language which ensures that speakers do not pronounce words like *huge* with initial [ʃ] because of the way they are spelled. Furthermore, in many non-standard accents of English it is very common for speakers to omit the initial [h] in such words, so that words like *huge* and *humour* are pronounced with initial [j]. But, while this change is not common in accents of English, it is found in Scots. For instance, in the Linguistic Survey of Scots, the item *huge* elicited numerous responses with [ʃ-]. It is also recorded in affectionate pronunciations of the personal names *Hugh, Hughie, Shoo(ey)* and *Shug/Shuggie*.

So, the ME spelling evidence points to a change from [h-] > [ç] > [ʃ], a phonetically plausible development, which is paralleled in certain northern place names and in some modern Scots dialects. There still remains the problem of the following vowel. Older Scots and northern ME texts have the form *sho*, whereas southern varieties have a spelling with <e>. The best solution to this problem that has so far been proposed is that it was derived by analogy with the masculine pronoun *he*.

Compared with the complexity presented by the evidence for the feminine pronoun, the masculine and neuter singular pronouns are relatively straightforward. Initial [h] is a very unstable sound in English and it has been lost in many accents of English, so it is unsurprising to find the OE neuter pronoun *hit* appearing as *it* in the ME period. Given that pronouns are generally unstressed, the initial [h] would have been even more prone to loss, though it is interesting to note that it does continue to appear sporadically until the end of the sixteenth century, when it vanishes from written English.

The reason for the replacement of the OE possessive neuter pronoun *his* with *its* was presumably an attempt to avoid confusion with the masculine possessive pronoun *his*, although it is striking that *its* does not appear until the sixteenth century. Up till that point there is no apparent need for a different pronoun for the masculine and neuter possessives. The origins of the form *its* are refreshingly straightforward: it is formed by adding a genitive <-s> inflexion to the nominative form *it*. Just as one adds an <-s> to a noun to make it possessive, so one adds an <-s> to a pronoun to make it possessive.

When *its* first appeared it was perceived as being colloquial and consequently was avoided by many formal writers. The Authorized Version of the Bible uses *his* exclusively, as in the following:

Ye are the salt of the earth: but if the salt have lost his savour, wherewith shall it be salted? (Matthew, 5:13)

Shakespeare mainly used *his*; the form *its* does not appear in any copy of his works published during his lifetime, although there are a handful of examples of *it's*, and one of *its*, in the plays first printed in the folio of 1623. This has led to the speculation that it is not his form at all, but a form added by his editors after his death. Intriguingly the few instances that do appear are all in plays written late in Shakespeare's career, which may indicate that he began to use the form late on in his life, once it had become fashionable and acceptable in Elizabethan usage. The following is an example of *it's* appearing in the copy of *The Tempest* printed in the First Folio:

> ... and my trust,
> Like a good parent, did beget him
> A falsehood in it's contrary as great
> As my trust was ...
>
> (*Twelfth Night*, 1.2.93–6)

An alternative possessive neuter pronoun also appears in Shakespeare's works: an endingless form *it*. The significance of this form for Shakespeare is unclear, although some of its uses suggest that it may have been a variant that was reserved for cases where the gender, or even the nature, of the referent was uncertain (Adamson, 2001). As an example we might consider the following exchange in *Hamlet* following Horatio's encounter with the Ghost in Act 1:

Hamlet: Did you not speak to it?
Horatio: My lord, I did,
But answer made it none; yet once methought
If lifted up it head and did address
Itself to motion, like as it would speak;

(*Hamlet*, 1.2.214–17)

Despite having recognized the ghost's likeness to the late king Hamlet, Horatio is clearly uncertain as to what kind of spirit it is and it is perhaps for this reason that he uses the pronoun *it* in this context. Later on in *Hamlet* there is another instance of *it* as the neuter possessive pronoun, and once again its use relates to a being of uncertain status: the corpse of Ophelia. The use of *it* was perhaps felt appropriate for a corpse of unknown identity, although of course this later proves ironic as the corpse is that of Ophelia.

This uninflected neuter pronoun is first recorded in the late fourteenth century in the north-western dialect of ME in the poems by the *Gawain*-poet, as in this example from *Pearl*:

I wan to a water by schore þat scherez
Lorde, dere watz hit adubbement!

There is a single example of this form in the Authorized Version of the Bible, although this instance was corrected to *its* in the 1660 and subsequent editions:

That which groweth of it own accord of thy harvest thou shalt not reap, neither gather the grapes of thy vine undressed: for it is a year of rest unto the land. (Leviticus 25:5)

This form did not achieve widespread adoption and soon died out in the standard language, although it is still used today in some north-western and northern dialects.

Alongside *its*, there were alternative periphrastic methods of marking the neuter possessive using *of*, namely *therof* and *of it*, which first appeared in ME and continued to be used throughout the EModE period. *Thereof* was frequent in late ME and survived as an alternative possessive neuter right up till the seventeenth century, when it became rare in most registers. The following quotation from the Authorized Version of the Bible shows the periphrastic genitive in use:

> And out of the ground the LORD God formed every beast of the field, and every fowl of the air; and brought them unto Adam to see what he would call them: and whatsoever Adam called every living creature, that was the name thereof. (Genesis 2:19)

The problems we observed above concerning the feminine pronoun *heo* following the monophthongization of the OE diphthongs also affected the third person plural pronouns. As a consequence of this sound change the OE nominative form *hīe* became *hī*, thus causing potential confusion with both the masculine and feminine third person singular pronouns. This potential for confusion was overcome by the introduction of a new form *þey/þay*; like the *she* pronoun adopted for the feminine pronoun, this form had the advantage of beginning with a different consonant sound altogether. This form is first recorded in the EME period, in the *Ormulum*, which has the nominative form *þeʒʒ*. Not only does this text have a new form for the nominative pronoun but it also has a new genitive form, *þeʒʒre*, and a less common alternative oblique form *þeʒʒm*. The fact that the *Ormulum* is an East Midland text alerts us to a possible Norse origin for these new pronouns, and this is confirmed by comparison with the equivalent form in ON. Despite the potential confusion we have noted in the nominative pronoun inherited from OE, and the early adoption of the Norse pronouns in the East Midlands, these forms were not adopted in the southern dialects of ME until the fourteenth century. Their appearance in the London dialect correlates with the adoption of other northern dialect features and with a period of large-scale immigration into London, especially from the northern counties (see the discussion in Chapter 3). When these pronouns do finally appear in London English, their adoption is gradual. Rather than adopting all three pronouns as a unit, London English appears to have taken in the nominative pronoun at first, while the *their* and *them* pronouns were not accepted until the early fifteenth century. This is well illustrated by Chaucer's usage, where we see the Norse-derived nominative pronoun *they*, alongside the OE derived pronouns *her* and *hem*. It seems that the requirement for a distinctive pronoun form applied only to the nominative case, perhaps because this form showed the greatest potential for confusion, and because the nominative case marks the subject of the sentence. Chaucer used the *their* and *them* pronouns just once throughout his work: in the northern dialect speech of the two students in the *Reeve's Tale*. This single instance shows us that, while these forms were evidently known in London English of this period, they were still considered to be northernisms, despite the fact that the nominative pronoun had by that date been accepted as a regular feature of the London dialect. By the early fifteenth century *their* and *them* had become fully integrated and all three pronouns are common in documents written in Samuels's Type 4 variety of London English, 'Chancery Standard' (see the discussion in Chapter 3). *They, their* and *them* became firmly established in the standard language in the EModE period, although, in some modern dialects and in informal spoken use, an unaccented form /əm/ was used, a descendant of OE *heom*, ME *hem*, showing that this form survived in dialect speech throughout the ME period, despite the pressure of the standard.

6.7 Further reading

In this chapter we have looked in detail at the changes that have taken place in the English grammatical system which transformed a language that relied heavily on inflexional endings to indicate case and number to a language that makes very little use of such endings. In trying to explain such a radical shift in structure we have seen that a number of contributing factors affected the change: changes in pronunciation, contact with different languages, principally the Scandinavian and French languages, contact between different dialects of English and sociolinguistic factors such as politeness. These examples help to demonstrate the 'multifactorial' nature of language change: language change is the result of a complex interaction of various linguistic and sociolinguistic factors and cannot be said to have a single cause.

All histories of the language include discussions of the issues covered in this chapter. For detailed treatment of individual periods see the sections dealing with morphology in the relevant volumes of the *Cambridge History of the English Language*. The loss of grammatical gender is the subject of Jones (1988); for a more recent discussion see Curzan (2003). The account of the development of the *she* pronoun given here is based upon that offered by Britton (1991). For a theoretical discussion of the T/V distinction in the second pronoun system see the work of Brown and Gilman (1960). Burnley (1983) has a useful discussion of the distinction between *thou* and *ye* in ME, while Wales (1983, 1985) focus on the EModE evidence.

Corpus Studies   7

In this book we have considered a range of approaches to the study of the history of English and investigated a series of case studies. In this chapter I want to build upon this foundation to suggest some ways by which this material can be taken further by those wishing to undertake research of this kind for themselves. One of the key developing areas in the field of English historical linguistics is that of corpus studies and there are number of resources currently available. In this chapter I want to highlight a selection of the most relevant of these resources and consider how they might be used to revisit some of the research questions addressed in this book.

One important recent development has been the digitization of historical dictionaries, allowing these resources to be interrogated in a variety of ways that are impossible in a print version. The *Oxford English Dictionary* is now available online in its second edition, while the ongoing third edition is being published in instalments via the world wide web. There are also separate dictionaries available for Old and Middle English, providing much more detailed and comprehensive coverage of these periods. The *Dictionary of Old English* is still under development, although a third of the dictionary has been completed and is available via the web. Also published as part of the dictionary project is an electronic text collection containing the entire OE corpus which can be searched for instances of individual words or phrases. The *Middle English Dictionary* was completed in 2001 and is now available in both print and electronic formats, as part of *The Middle English Compendium*. The online version of the dictionary facilitates a range of different types of searches, allowing a user to search individual entries and quotations as well as headwords. In addition to the online version of the dictionary, the *Middle English Compendium* offers its users access to a corpus of ME texts which can be searched for further occurrences of individual words, using simple, proximity and boolean searches. However, given that there are many more

ME than OE texts, this corpus is necessarily a selection, rather than a comprehensive collection, of all texts written in ME. The corpus draws heavily on editions that are out of copyright, although these are not always the most reliable basis for a philological analysis. In this book I have emphasized the importance of dealing with primary evidence, whereas edited texts are ones which have been subjected to some form of editorial intervention. The degree of intervention often differs according to the prejudices of the editor, the audience for which it was intended and the conventions of the publisher responsible for printing the edition. It is therefore important to be aware of potential differences in editorial practices across the various editions included in this and similar text corpora.

There are corpora available that represent the manuscript more faithfully and which are more suitable for analysis of features of orthography, phonology and morphology. For instance, a database of the more than two hundred and fifty texts copied in the eleventh century provides the foundation for studies of the transitional phase between Old and Middle English, enabling searching of spellings of individual words or stems. As well as searching the complete corpus, it is possible to obtain results which break down the results of searches into chronological sequences so that one can see whether the distribution of a form varies across the period represented by the corpus. This database has also made available a classification of characteristic graphetic, or handwriting, features associated with individual 'scriptors': scribes responsible for producing multiple copies of the texts represented in this corpus. One potential use of this resource is to enable us to examine how widespread forms associated with the Late West Saxon variety were in the eleventh century. In Chapter 3 we saw how this particular dialect became established as a standard variety of OE, being used by scribes throughout the country in preference to their own local dialect. However, we also saw that features of Late West Saxon often appear alongside a mixture of non-West Saxon forms, complicating the picture of its status and influence. We can, however, draw upon this corpus to establish a clearer picture of how widespread Late West Saxon was during this period, and to detail its geographical and chronological spread. To give you an example of how this kind of analysis might be conducted, let us examine the distribution of a single feature that is characteristic of Late West Saxon: the spelling <ea>, reflecting a diphthongal pronunciation, the result of a sound change known as 'breaking', where other dialects have <a>, e.g *eald* 'old', *ealdor* 'lord' vs non-West Saxon *ald*, *aldor*. The distribution of these spellings in the corpus convincingly demonstrates the dominance of the Late West Saxon form: there are in excess of 2500 instances of *eald-* against just 38 examples of *ald-*. A similar ratio is found, although on a smaller scale, in the case of the adjective *beald/bald* 'bold'. In this case the Late West Saxon spelling *beald* is recorded in 70 instances, while the non-West Saxon spelling *bald* is limited to just six occurrences. Using the corpus in this way it would be possible to construct a much bigger profile of such distinctions in order to build up a fine-grained picture of the adoption of late West Saxon forms throughout the country during the late OE period, and to identify areas where its influence seems to have been less decisive.

Electronic resources for the study of the transition from Old to Middle English have been further increased by the recent online publication of the first phase of the *Linguistic Atlas of Early Middle English*, the daughter project of the *Linguistic Atlas of Late Mediaeval English* published in printed form in 1986 and discussed in Chapter 2. LAEME is now available online in a revised format, although further revisions are projected before the process of publication is completed. LAEME is designed to complement its parent atlas by providing dialect information about the period immediately before that covered by LALME, that is 1150–325. However, because of the comparatively smaller number of texts that survive from the earlier period, LAEME differs from LALME in analysing all the available material rather than limiting itself to sample tranches of texts. To carry out such an analysis the LAEME editors transcribed all the relevant texts into electronic form and assigned each word a lexico-grammatical tag that provides information about its meaning and part of speech. The resulting transcription can be viewed as a marked-up text or as a 'text dictionary', providing a full listing of all the words in a particular text accompanied by their Present-day English reflex and relevant grammatical information. This tagging system is extremely helpful in allowing a user to search for all instances of a particular PDE word, irrespective of its ME reflexes, as well as searching for occurrences of particular ME spelling forms. In addition to searching for individual words it is also possible to identify multiple instances of particular morphemes, such as the third person singular present indicative ending, the prefix *for-* or the suffix *-dom* for instance.

One of the advantages of this kind of resource is that it enables us to contextualize the usages of certain scribes within a much more extensive corpus of contemporary linguistic data. As an example of the kinds of searching that are made possible by this new resource we might reconsider the case of AB language, discussed in chapter 3. In our earlier discussion we noted that there has been a tendency among scholars to view this variety as a standard language, despite a certain amount of inconsistency and irregularity between the two manuscripts that employ this variety. But more significant for its status as a standard variety was the question of its influence: how many other scribes adopted features characteristic of AB language. So far this question has been addressed in a partial and impressionistic way, because of the lack of data upon which the question may be considered. But using the LAEME corpus it is possible to search for individual features that are characteristic of AB language to see how widespread they were among contemporary scribes.

As a preliminary investigation I searched the LAEME database for a small selection of features that are typical of AB language, to determine how widely they were employed by other scribes of this period. The features chosen for examination were: <hw> in words like *hwet* 'what', spellings showing <e> for West Saxon <æ>, a result of the sound change known as 'second fronting', e.g. *wes* 'was', *dei* 'day', *efter* 'after', spellings with a rounded <o> instead of the more common <a> spelling before nasal consonants, e.g. *mon* 'man', and the characteristic AB use of <ea> to represent the short front vowel usually spelled <æ>, e.g. *heard* 'hard'. Some of these features were found to be comparatively well attested throughout the corpus. For instance, there are 474 occurrences of the spelling *mon*, appearing in 55 separate texts, showing that this feature was fairly common throughout the Western dialects. Spellings showing 'second fronting' are found to be particularly associated with text connected with the AB manuscripts; there are a large number of such forms in copies of the *Ancrene Riwle* and in other Katherine Group texts such as *Hali Meiðhad* and *Sawles Warde*. They are, however, not limited to this network of closely related texts, nor are they exclusive to the Western dialects. There are occurrences of *dei* 'day' in Eastern texts such as the *Peterborough Chronicle* and a manuscript localized to Norfolk. The spelling *efter* 'after' is recorded in the south-east, both in the *Kentish Sermons* and the *Ayenbite of Inwyt* by Dan Michel, a monk of Canterbury. Related spellings are ones with <eo> instead of <e>, showing a subsequent change known as 'back mutation'. Spellings showing this development appear to be more limited in their distribution. For instance, all occurrences of the verb 'eat' spelled *eot* are recorded in *Ancrene Riwle* or Katherine Group texts, with just two exceptions: single occurrence in Cotton Otho C.XIII of Laȝamon's *Brut*, localized by LAEME to south-west Wiltshire, and the *Lambeth Homilies*, localized to North-West Worcestershire and therefore geographically close to the AB heartland. The unusual spelling *heard* 'hard' is rarely attested in the corpus, as we would expect, although interestingly it is recorded outside the AB manuscripts. There are occurrences in BL MS Cotton Caligula A.IX of Laȝamon's *Brut* and in the copy of Ælfric's grammar in Worcester Cathedral Library F.174, in the hand of a scribe associated with Worcester Cathedral Priory, known as the 'tremulous' scribe on account of his characteristically shaky handwriting. Much more analysis of this kind would be needed to construct a detailed profile of how widespread these AB features were, and in which dialects they can be found, but LAEME provides us with powerful tools which make this kind of analysis possible.

The completion of LAEME, and the availability of the new tools developed as part of this project, has led to the establishment of a further project to produce an electronic version of LALME, although this project is still underway. Another attempt to build on the fruits of the LALME project is a collaborative venture at the Universities of Glasgow and Stavangar, Norway, which aim to produce an up-to-date description of ME orthography, morphology and phonology. In order to achieve this goal the first stage of this project has been the assembly of a searchable electronic corpus of 3000 word tranches of all texts localized by LALME. This corpus is being made available to other researchers online; at present approximately a third of such texts are available, although the corpus is being updated at six-month intervals.

Other electronic resources that are relevant to the study of late ME are editions of the works of literary authors such as Chaucer and Langland. The *Piers Plowman Electronic Archive* is producing CD-ROM editions of all of the surviving manuscripts of Langland's poem, providing access to full colour digital images and searchable texts transcribed directly from the manuscripts. *The Canterbury Tales Project* has a similar goal, although this project is releasing CD-ROMs that focus on single tales rather than individual manuscripts. The advantage of this approach for the student of ME is that it is possible to search a particular text across all fifty-eight manuscript and pre-1500 printed witnesses of the *Canterbury Tales*. Given that the manuscripts of the *Canterbury Tales* were copied throughout the fifteenth century, these electronic transcripts provide a very useful resource for tracing the process of standardization of spelling. In Chapter 3 we considered the process by which 'Chancery Standard' was disseminated from offices of state such as the Chancery and how it became adopted more widely by writers such as the members of the Paston family. We also saw that there is considerable scholarly debate concerning the relative importance of 'Chancery Standard' in the process of standardization, and the speed with which a standard language was established. To resolve these disputes we need detailed analyses of the diffusion of Chancery spellings across a range of different types of text. The electronic texts produced by the *Piers Plowman Archive* and the *Canterbury Tales Project* provide useful resources for tracing this development, and the extent to which scribes copying literary manuscripts throughout this period were influenced by the practices being adopted in the Chancery and other offices of state. An exploratory study of this kind has been carried out by N.F. Blake (1997), who found that Chancery forms were much less common among the fifteenth-century copies of the Wife of Bath's Prologue than might have been expected. A further analysis that I carried out on the same corpus of manuscripts showed that many of Chaucer's scribes were concerned with preserving features of the author's own dialect, Type III London English, rather than adopting the forms characteristic of Chancery Standard (Horobin, 2003). More studies of this kind would help to fill out the picture of fifteenth-century spelling practices, and enable us to trace the process of standardization with greater precision.

As we saw in Chapter 2, the late ME and EModE periods saw the expansion of the vernacular to encompass a much wider diversity of text types than in the early ME period. It is therefore important that we do not limit our-selves to the study of literary texts in tracing developments in the English language throughout these periods. To enable a more comprehensive study of Middle and Early Modern English a number of specialized corpora have been developed that focus on specific text types, such as medical and sci-entific writing, religious writing and so on. A number of such corpora have been produced at the Research Unit for Variation, Contacts and Change in English (VARIENG), based at the University of Helsinki. The *Helsinki Corpus: Diachronic and Dialectal* was one of the earliest historical corpora, allowing searching across a range of texts produced between *c.* 750 to *c.* 1700. More recent additions to the suite of Helsinki corpora include collections of Early English Correspondence and Early English Medical Writing, as well as the records associated with the Salem Witchcraft trials. The *Corpus of Early English Correspondence* comprises 2.7 million words made up of letters dated from 1417 to 1681, although since its completion in 1998 this corpus has been extended to cover a greater diachronic range and expanded to give increased coverage to the time periods initially covered. The usefulness of letters for carrying out socio-historical linguistic studies was discussed in Chapter 3, where we looked at some examples from the letters of the Pas-ton family. This much-larger sample enables similar kinds of analysis to be carried out over a more extended period, using texts that are firmly dated and localized and whose authors are known. As with the Paston letters, the *Corpus of Early English Correspondence* contains much less data on women's language, given their lack of literacy during the period. The *Corpus of Early English Medical Writing* was published in 2005 and contains a collection of 500,000 words taken from medical treatises written between 1375–1800. The editors of this corpus have also published a number of studies that demonstrate the importance of such a collection for our understanding of the development of the language during this period. Focusing on the period 1375–1550, Taavitsainen (2000) carried out a preliminary analysis of the spelling practices revealed in the documents copied during this period to observe the process of standardization across these texts. Rather than con-firming the widespread influence of Chancery Standard forms, her results identified the continued importance of the Central Midlands Standard, Samuels Type I. These findings further complicate the picture surrounding the dissemination of Chancery Standard while also shedding new light on our understanding of Central Midlands Standard. In Chapter 3 we saw that Samuels first identified this variety as common in manuscripts associated with John Wycliffe and his followers, known as the Lollards. Taavitsainen's findings show that this type of language was more widespread than Samuels suggested, and that it was common in scientific as well as religious texts. These preliminary findings need further exploration to consider the origins of this variety and the extent of its influence across a variety of further text types.

So far we have focused on the uses of such corpora for the analysis of spelling forms, although the subsequent implementation of syntactic annotation has resulted in the publication of corpora that are very useful for the study of syntax of both the ME and EModE periods. The syntactic parsing that has been added to these corpora, to produce the Penn-Helsinki Parsed Corpora of Middle English and Early Modern English (PPCEME) allows the corpora to be searched not just for individual words but also for sequences of words and for syntactic structure.

The publication of the *OED* in electronic format, both on CD-ROM and online, is transforming the way in which this resource can be manipulated for the study of the development of the English lexicon. Instead of simply looking up entries under individual headwords, it is now possible to search the dictionary in a range of complex ways. For instance, it is possible to search entries according to particular authors, giving us access to the number of times an author provides the earliest recorded use of a word, or the number of nonce words, words that appear just once, that are found in a particular writer's works. Using the advanced search engine on the *OED* online we can identify that there are, for instance, 1986 first citations taken from the works of Chaucer. By contrast, William Langland, one of Chaucer's contemporaries, appears just 122 times amongst the first citations. The works of John Gower, another fourteenth-century poet, are responsible for 464 first citations: more than Langland but nothing like as many as are taken from Chaucer. Such figures are interesting, although we do need to be cautious about how we interpret them. It is tempting to imagine that the large number of first occurrences found in Chaucer's works is an index of his linguistic novelty, and a demonstration of the way that he sought to enrich the English language by introducing numerous borrowings from the stylistically more elevated languages, especially French and Latin. There are, however, many other factors that might influence these results. The fact that Chaucer's works were widely available and valued for their literary merit certainly influenced the extent to which his texts were mined for quotations in the making of the *OED*, and this has undoubtedly contributed to the large number of first citations. We must also remember that the lack of earlier attestations may simply be historical accident, or may be the result of an incomplete reading of surviving ME materials by *OED* editors. The recent completion of the MED, with its much more comprehensive coverage of the ME period, has revealed numerous earlier attestations of words whose first occurrence is attributed to Chaucer in the second edition of the *OED* (Cannon, 1998). Perhaps more interesting in terms of judging Chaucer's novelty, and the extent to which words used by him were subsequently adopted by later writers, is to examine the afterlife of the words first recorded in his works. For instance, of the 1986 first citations in Chaucer's works, 136 are 'nonce' words: words which do not appear again in any subsequent text and therefore made little impact upon the English language. These nonce words act as a useful reminder that not all words first recorded in Chaucer's works made an impact upon the English language, and thus force us to reconsider the view that Chaucer's language was instrumental in establishing English as a prestigious literary language.

In addition to searching the dictionary to elicit information about particular writers and citations taken from their works it is also possible to search the definitions, enabling us to use the dictionary as a kind of thesaurus. We saw in Chapter 5 that studies of how words change their meaning cannot be carried out in isolation, so that it is important to be able to identify all words within a particular semantic field. It is therefore helpful to be able to search the *OED* to identify groups of words with a similar range of meaning. As an example we might search for all words used by Chaucer that include the word 'proud' in their definition, which gives us a list of synonyms that includes *arrogant, digne, deignous, hautein, insolent, proud, vain*. This kind of research will be further facilitated by the appearance of the *Historical Thesaurus of English*, now available online and due for publication in print format in late 2009. To consider further the uses of a thesaurus based upon the data provided by the *OED* for the study of semantic change, I want to look at a single example of a word that has changed its meaning quite considerably throughout its history: the adjective *sad*.

In OE the adjective *sad* meant 'full' or 'satisfied' whereas today it is used to refer to an unhappy state of mind. How did this change come about? If we look up this word in the *OED* we find the following definitions:

1. Having had one's fill; satisfied, sated; weary or tired (of something).
   OE–1500
2. Settled, firmly established in purpose or condition; steadfast, firm, constant.
   1340–1667
3. Of looks, appearance: dignified, grave, serious.
   1375–1798
4. Unmistakable, certain; true, genuine.
   1400–1475

A second group of senses falls under the general heading 'Feeling sorrow or regret, and related uses', and this is the meaning that has survived into PDE. This use is first recorded in the fourteenth century and thus appears to over-lap with the earliest uses of the word in senses 2–4. It is clear from the dates given in the *OED* entries that the ME period saw the greatest expansion in the use of this word, but this does not help explain why these additional senses became attached to the word. If we compare the development found in this word throughout the history of English with its use in other Germanic languages then we can see that the development of the modern sense is unique to English. The word originally derives from an Indo-European root meaning 'satisfy', the same root from which the Latin *satis* descends, and there are equivalent words in modern Germanic languages, such as modern German *satt* which means 'full, well-fed'.

To understand the series of changes that the word *sad* underwent during its history we need to consider the uses of other words with related meanings. Let us begin by considering the meaning 'full, satiated' which fell out of use by 1500. A search of the *Historical Thesaurus* identifies a number of words with this meaning, with their dates of use as recorded in the *OED*:

sad	OE–1450
full	1297–1625
saturate	1550–1604
cloyed	1611–1712
satiate	1667–1781
surfeit	1699–1877
sated	1699–1873
full up (of)	1890

This search reveals that there have been a number of synonyms for this word throughout the history of English, so that it is likely that the interaction between these words and *sad* is at least partly responsible for the change in meaning found in that word. Of particular significance is the appearance of *satiate* in the seventeenth century as an adjective, but recorded earlier as a verb. The earliest recorded use of this word in *OED* is under the headword *satiate* (past participle), where it appears in a text dated to 1440: 'þai war saciatt & fulfyllid þerwith as it had bene with meate or drynk'. This word is a borrowing from Latin *satiatus*, the past participle of *satiare* 'to satiate', and its appearance in English in the late ME period is part of the process of borrowing from Latin that was common in the fifteenth and sixteenth centuries. In the sixteenth century another loanword from Latin appeared with similar meaning, *saturate*, derived from Latin *saturatus*, the past participle of *saturare*.

This overlap in meaning between these two Latin loans and the adjective *sad* helps to explain the loss of the meaning 'satisfied', 'full', but it still leaves unexplained the corresponding change of meaning. If there was no longer any use for the word *sad*, why did it continue to be used, and how did the

PDE sense of 'feeling sorrow or regret' develop? If we look back at the earliest examples of this word then we can see that, as well as referring to the physical sense of being 'full', *sad* can also refer to an emotional sense of fullness: a weariness or tedium towards something. During the ME period this use widened considerably, so that we find *sad* used to describe someone who is 'steadfast', 'firm', 'grave', 'serious' and 'genuine'. There is a clear link between these senses and the modern meaning 'feeling sorrow or regret', in that a grave and serious expression may well be interpreted as one that expresses sorrow or regret. This is apparent from the quotations presented in the *OED* entry, some of which could be assigned to either category. The following example is listed under the heading 'sorrowful, mournful', although it could potentially be listed under the heading 'grave, serious': 'Malancoly he was of complexioun, ... Soroufull, sadde, ay dreidfull, but plesance.' In contrast the quotation 'Their brow, besprent with thin hairs, white as snow, ... Whilst on their sad looks smilingly, they bear The trace of creeping age' is placed under 'grave, serious', even though it could equally well fit under 'sorrowful, mournful'. This example shows how the combination of the electronic *OED* and the *Historical Thesaurus* can be used to enable much more detailed understanding of the processes by which words have changed their meaning, both individually and as part of larger semantic networks.

7.1 **Further reading**

In this chapter we have surveyed some of the most relevant electronic resources that are currently available either online or in CD-ROM format and have considered a sample of the research questions that they can be used to address. For a more general introduction to Corpus studies and its use in linguistics more widely you should consult Biber, Conrad and Reppen (1999). The *OED* online can be accessed at http://dictionary.oed.com, the *Middle English Compendium* site is http://quod.lib.umich.edu/m/mec and the *Dictionary of Old English* and its associated corpus of texts is available from http://www.doe.utoronto.ca/. All of these publications require an institutional or individual subscription. The *Manchester Inventory of Script and Spellings in Eleventh-Century English* can be accessed freely at http://www.arts. manchester.ac.uk/mancass/C11database/. The *Linguistic Atlas of Early Middle English* is also freely available, along with detailed introductory material explaining how the database was compiled and its various search facilities http://www.lel.ed.ac.uk/ihd/laeme1/laeme1.html. The ongoing *Middle English Grammar Project* maintains a website which allows access to the corpus as well as details of the larger project and links to associated publications: http://www.uis.no/research/culture/the_middle_english_grammar_project/meg-c/.

The Canterbury Tales Project has issued a total of seven CD-ROMs to date covering various prologues and tales, as well as a digital facsimile of the Hengwrt manuscript including a searchable transcript of both this and the Ellesmere manuscript. Details of these and future publications can be found on their website: http://www.canterburytalesproject.org/. *The Piers Plowman Electronic Archive* has so far published six CD-ROM facsimiles of manuscripts of the poem, details of which can be found on the project website: http://www.iath.virginia.edu/seenet/piers/.

Details of the completed and ongoing Helsinki corpus projects can be obtained from the website of the Research Unit for Variation, Contacts and Change in English: http://www.helsinki.fi/varieng/index.html, while the parsed versions of the corpora can be purchased on CD-ROM via the following link: http://www.ling.upenn.edu/hist-corpora/. The *Historical Thesaurus of English* is currently accessible online but will subsequently also be available in print: http://libra.englang.arts.gla.ac.uk/historicalthesaurus/.

Bibliography

Adams, Valerie, *An Introduction to Modern English Word Formation* (London: Longman, 1973).

Adamson, Sylvia, 'Understanding Shakespeare's Grammar: Studies in Small Words', in *Reading Shakespeare's Dramatic Language: A Guide*, ed., Sylvia Adamson et al. (London: Thomson, 2001), 210–36.

Aitchison, Jean, *Language Change: Progress or Decay?* 3rd edition (Cambridge: Cambridge University Press, 2001).

———, *The Language Web: The Power and Problem of Words* (Cambridge: Cambridge University Press, 2001).

Barber, Charles, *Early Modern English* (Edinburgh: Edinburgh University Press, 1997).

———, *The English Language: A Historical Introduction* (Cambridge: Cambridge University Press, 1993).

———, '"You" and "Thou" in Shakespeare's Richard III', *Leeds Studies in English* 12 (1981), 273–89.

Baugh, A.C. and T. Cable, *A History of the English Language*, 5th edition (London: Routledge, 2001).

Bennett, J.A.W. and G.V. Smithers (eds), *Early Middle English Verse and Prose* (Oxford: Clarendon Press, 1968).

Benskin, Michael, 'Chancery Standard', in *New Perspectives on English Historical Linguistics: Selected papers from 12 ICEHL. Volume II: Lexis and Transmission*, eds, Christian J. Kay, Carole Hough and Irené Wotherspoon (Amsterdam: Benjamins, 2004), 1–40.

———, 'The Fit-technique explained,' in *Regionalism in Late Medieval Manuscripts and Texts*, ed., Felicity Riddy (Cambridge: D.S. Brewer, 1991), 9–26.

———, 'The letters <þ> and <y> in later Middle English, and some related matters', *Journal of the Society of Archivists* 7 (1982), 13–30.

Biber, D., S. Conrad and R. Reppen, *Corpus Linguistics. Investigating Language Structure and Use* (Cambridge, Cambridge University Press, 1998).

Black, Merja, 'AB or Simply A? Reconsidering the Case for a Standard', *Neuphilologische Mitteilungen* 100 (1999), 155–74.

Blake, N.F., 'Chancery English and the Wife of Bath's Prologue' in *To Explain the Present: Studies in the Changing English Language in Honour of Matti Rissanen*, ed.,

Terttu Nevalainen and Leena Kahlas Tarkka (Helsinki: Société Néophilologique, 1997), 3–24.

Blake, N.F., *A History of the English Language* (Basingstoke: Macmillan, 1996).

—— (ed.), *The Cambridge History of the English Language Volume II 1066–1476* (Cambridge: Cambridge University Press, 1992).

——, *William Caxton and English Literary Culture* (London: Hambledon, 1991).

——, *The English Language in Medieval Literature* (London: Dent, 1977, 1979).

——, *Caxton's Own Prose* (London: Deutsch, 1973).

——, *Caxton and His World* (London: Deutsch, 1969).

Bowers, J.M., 'Hoccleve's Two Copies of *Lerne to Dye*: Implications for Textual Critics', *Papers of the Bibliographical Society of America* 83 (1989), 437–72.

Britton, Derek, 'On ME *she/sho*: a Scots solution to an English problem', *Nowele [North-Western European Language Evolution]* 17 (1991), 3–51.

Brown, Roger and Albert Gilman, 'The pronouns of power and solidarity', in *Style in Language* Thomas A. Sebeok (ed.) (Cambridge, MA: Massachusetts Institute of Technology, 1960), 253–76.

Burnley, David, *The History of the English Language: A Sourcebook*, 2nd edition (London: Longman, 2000).

——, 'Lexis and Semantics' in Blake 1992, 409–99.

——, *A Guide to Chaucer's Language* (Basingstoke: Macmillan, 1983).

Burrow, J.A. (ed.) (1999), *Thomas Hoccleve's Complaint and Dialogue* Early English Text Society OS 313 (Oxford: Oxford University Press).

——, *Thomas Hoccleve*. Authors of the Middle Ages 4 (Aldershot: Variorum, 1994).

Campbell, A., *Old English Grammar* (Oxford: Clarendon Press 1959).

Cannon, Christopher, *The Making of Chaucer's English: A Study of Words* (Cambridge: Cambridge University Press, 1998).

Chambers, R.W. and M. Daunt (eds), *A Book of London English 1384–1425* (Oxford: Clarendon Press, 1931).

Clanchy, M.T., *From Memory to Written Record: England 1066–1307* (London, 1979).

Clark, Cecily, 'The Myth of "the Anglo-Norman Scribe"' in *History of Englishes: New Methods and Interpretations in Historical Linguistics*, eds, Matti Rissanen, Ossi Ihalainen, Terttu Nevalainen, Irma Taavitsainen (Berlin: Mouton de Gruyter, 1992).

——, 'Another Late-Fourteenth-Century Case of Dialect-Awareness', *English Studies* 62 (1981), 504–5.

Curzan Anne, *Gender Shifts in the History of English* (Cambridge: Cambridge University Press, 2003).

Cusack, Bridget, *Everyday English, 1500–1700: A Reader* (Edinburgh: Edinburgh University Press, 1999).

Dance, R., 'The AB Language: the Recluse, the Gossip and the Language Historian', in *A Companion to Ancrene Wisse*, ed., Y. Wada (Cambridge: D.S. Brewer, 2003), 57–82.

Davis, Norman, 'The Language of two brothers in the fifteenth century,' in *Five Hundred Years of Words and Sounds: A Festschrift for Eric Dobson*, eds, Eric Stanley and Douglas Gray (D.S. Brewer: Cambridge, 1983), 23–8.

Dobson, E.J., *English Pronunciation 1500–1700* (Oxford: Oxford University Press, 1968).

Dobson, E.J., 'Early Modern Standard English', *Transactions of the Philological Society* (1955), 25–54.

Doyle, A.I. and M.B. Parkes, 'The Production of Copies of the *Canterbury Tales* and the *Confessio Amantis* in the Early Fifteenth Century', in *Medieval Scribes, Manuscripts, and Libraries: Essays Presented to N.R. Ker*, eds, M.B. Parkes and A.G. Watson (London: Scolar Press, 1978), 163–210.

Fisher, John H., *The Emergence of Standard English* (Kentucky: University Press, 1996).

Gneuss, Helmut, 'The origin of Standard Old English and Æthelwold's school at Winchester', *Anglo-Saxon England* 1 (1972), 63–83.

Godden, M.R., 'Did King Alfred Write Anything?' *Medium Ævum* 76 (2007), 1–23.

Görlach, Manfred, *The Linguistic History of English* (Basingstoke: Palgrave Macmillan, 1994).

———, *An Introduction to Early Modern English* (Cambridge: Cambridge University Press, 1991).

———, *The Textual Tradition of the South English Legendary*, Leeds Texts and Monographs (Leeds: The University of Leeds, 1974).

Hogg, R., *An Introduction to Old English* (Edinburgh: Edinburgh University Press, 2002).

———, *A Grammar of Old English: Phonology* (Oxford: Blackwell, 1992a).

——— (ed.), *The Cambridge History of the English Language Volume I: The Beginnings to 1066* (Cambridge: Cambridge University Press, 1992b).

———, 'On the Impossibility of Old English dialectology', in *Luick Revisited*, eds, Dieter Kastovsky and Gero Bauer (Tübingen: G. Narr, 1988), 183–203.

Horobin, Simon, 'Chaucerian Word-Formation', *Neuphilologische Mitteilungen* 110 (2009), 141–57.

———, *Chaucer's Language* (Basingstoke: Palgrave Macmillan, 2006).

———, '"In London and opelond": The dialect and circulation of the C version of *Piers Plowman*', *Medium Ævum* 74 (2005), 248–69.

———, *The Language of the Chaucer Tradition* (Cambridge: D.S. Brewer, 2003).

Horobin, Simon and Linne R. Mooney, 'A *Piers Plowman* manuscript by the Hengwrt/ Ellesmere scribe and its implications for London Standard English', *Studies in the Age of Chaucer* 26 (2004), 65–112.

Horobin, Simon and Jeremy Smith, *An Introduction to Middle English* (Edinburgh: Edinburgh University Press, 2002).

Hudson, Richard, *Sociolinguistics* (Cambridge: Cambridge University Press, 1980).

Hughes, Geoffrey, *A History of English Words* (Oxford: Blackwell, 2000).

Jeffries, Lesley, *Discovering Language: The Structure of Modern English* (Basingstoke: Palgrave Macmillan, 2006).

Jones, C., *Grammatical Gender in English 950–1200* (London: Croom Helm, 1988).

Jordan, Richard, *Handbuch der mittelenglischen Grammatik: Lautlehre* (Heidelberg: Winter, 1925), trans. E.J. Crook (The Hague: Mouton, 1994).

Kaiser, R., *Zur Geographie des mittelenglischen Wortschatzes* (Leipzig: Mayer & Müller, 1937).

Kurath, H., S.M. Kuhn and R.E. Lewis (eds), *Middle English Dictionary* (Ann Arbor: University of Michigan Press, 1952–2001).

Labov, William, *Sociolinguistic Patterns* (Philadelphia: University of Pennsylvania Press, 1972).

Laing, Margaret, 'Confusion *WRS* confounded: Literal substitution sets in early Middle English writing systems', *Neuphilologische Mitteilungen* 100 (1999), 251–70.

——— (ed.), *Middle English Dialectology: Essays on Some Principles and Problems* (Aberdeen: Aberdeen University Press, 1989).

Laing, Margaret and Roger Lass (eds), *A Linguistic Atlas of Early Middle English, 1150–1325* (Edinburgh: The University of Edinburgh, 2007) [http://www.lel.ed.ac.uk/ihd/laeme1/laeme1.html]

Lakoff, George and Mark Johnson, *Metaphors We Live By* (Chicago: University of Chicago Press, 1980).

Lass, Roger (ed.), *The Cambridge History of the English Language Volume III: 1476–1776* (Cambridge: Cambridge University Press, 1999).

———, *Historical Linguistics and Language Change* (Cambridge: Cambridge University Press, 1997).

———, *Old English: A Historical Linguistic Companion* (Cambridge: Cambridge University Press, 1994).

Machan, Tim William, *English in the Middle Ages* (Oxford: Oxford University Press, 2003).

Marchand, H., *The Categories and Types of Present-day English Word-formation* 2nd edition (Munich: Beck, 1969).

McIntosh, A.I., M.L. Samuels and M. Benskin (eds), *A Linguistic Atlas of Late Mediaeval English* (Aberdeen: Aberdeen University Press, 1986), 4 vols.

McMahon, A.M.S., *Understanding Language Change* (Cambridge: Cambridge University Press, 1994).

Milroy, James, *Linguistic Variation and Change* (Oxford: Blackwell, 1992).

Milroy, J. and L. Milroy, *Authority in Language: Investigating Language Prescription and Standardisation* (London: Routledge, 1985).

Mooney, Linne R., 'Chaucer's Scribe', *Speculum* 81 (2006), 97–138.

Mustanoja, T., *A Middle English Syntax*, Vol. 1 (Helsinki: Société Néophilologique, 1959).

Mugglestone, L. (ed.), *The Oxford History of English* (Oxford: Oxford University Press, 2006).

———, *Talking Proper: The Rise of Accent as Social Symbol* (Oxford: Oxford University Press, 1995).

Nevalainen, Terttu, *An Introduction to Early Modern English* (Edinburgh: Edinburgh University Press, 2006).

———, 'Shakespeare's New Words', in *Reading Shakespeare's Dramatic Language: A Guide*, ed., Sylvia Adamson et al. (London: Thomson, 2001), 237–55.

Nevalainen, T. and H. Raumolin-Brunberg, 'Its strength and the beauty of it: the standardisation of the third person neuter possessive in Early Modern English' in *Towards a Standard English 1600–1800*, eds, D. Stein and I. Tieken-Boon van Ostade (Berlin, 1994), 171–216.

Osselton, N., 'Informal spelling systems in Early Modern English: 1500–1800', in *English Historical Linguistics: Studies in Development*, eds, N.F. Blake and C. Jones (Sheffield: CECTAL, 1984), 123–36.

———, 'Formal and informal spelling in the eighteenth century', *English Studies* 44 (1963), 267–75.

Oxford English Dictionary, 2nd edition (Oxford: Oxford University Press, 1989).

Page, R., *An Introduction to English Runes* (1973).

Platzer, Hans,'"No Sex Please, We're Anglo-Saxon?" On Grammatical Gender in Old English". *VIEW[Z]: Vienna English Working Papers* 10.1 (2001), 34–47.

Richardson, Malcolm, 'Henry V, the English Chancery, and Chancery English', *Speculum* 55 (1980), 726–50.

Sampson, Geoffrey, *Writing Systems* (London: Hutchinson, 1985).

Samuels, M.L., *Linguistic Evolution with Special Reference to English* (Cambridge: Cambridge University Press, 1972).

———, 'Some Applications of Middle English Dialectology', *English Studies*, 44 (1963), 81–94, reprinted in Margaret Laing (ed.), *Middle English Dialectology: Essays on Some Principles and Problems* (Aberdeen: Aberdeen University Press, 1989), 64–80.

Samuels, M.L. and Jeremy J. Smith, 'The Language of Gower', *Neuphilologische Mitteilungen* 82 (1981), 294–304, reprinted in *The English of Chaucer and His Contemporaries*, ed., J.J. Smith (Aberdeen: Aberdeen University Press, 1988), 13–22.

Sandved, A., 'Prolegomena to a renewed study of the rise of Standard English', in *So Meny People, Longages and Tonges*, eds, M. Benskin and M.L. Samuels (Edinburgh: MEDP, 1981), 31–42.

Scragg, D.G., *A History of English Spelling* (Manchester: Manchester University Press, 1974).

Serjeantson, M.S., *A History of Foreign Words in English* (London: Routledge & Kegan Paul, 1935, reprinted in 1961).

Shepherd, G., *Ancrene Wisse: Parts VI and VII* (Manchester: Manchester University Press, 1972).

Smith, Jeremy J., *Sound Change and the History of English* (Oxford: Oxford University Press, 2007).

———, 'Standard language in early middle English?' in *Placing Middle English in Context*, eds, I. Taavitsainen et al. (Berlin: Mouton de Gruyter, 2001), 125–39.

———, *An Historical Study of English: Function, Form and Change* (London: Routledge, 1996).

———, 'Spelling and tradition in fifteenth-century copies of Gower's *Confessio Amantis*', in *The English of Chaucer and His Contemporaries*, ed., J.J. Smith (Aberdeen: Aberdeen University Press, 1988), 96–113.

———, 'Some spellings in Caxton's Malory', *Poetica* 24 (1986), 58–63.

Stanley, Eric, 'Karl Luick's 'Man schrieb wie man sprach' and English Historical Philology', in *Luick Revisited*, eds, Dieter Kastovsky and Gero Bauer (Tübingen: G. Narr, 1988), 311–34.

Strang, Barbara M.H., *A History of English* (London: Methuen, 1970).

Taavitsainen, Irma, 'Scientific language and spelling standardisation', in L. Wright 2000, 131–54.

Tolkien, J.R.R., '*Ancrene Wisse* and *Hali Meiðhad*', *Essays and Studies* 14 (1929), 104–26.

Trotter, D.A. (ed.), *Multilingualism in Later Medieval Britain* (Cambridge: D.S. Brewer, 2000).

Turville-Petre, Thorlac, *England the Nation: Language, Literature, and National Identity 1290–1340* (Oxford: Clarendon Press, 1996).

Waldron, R.A., *Sense and Sense Development* (London: Deutsch, 1979).

Wales Katie, 'Generic 'your' and Jacobean drama: the rise and fall of a pronominal usage', *English Studies* 66 (1985), 7–24.

——, 'Thou and you in Early Modern English: Brown and Gilman revisited', *Studia Linguistica* 37 (1983), 107–25.

Wells, John, *Accents of English* (Cambridge: Cambridge University Press, 1982), 3 vols.

Wright, Laura (ed.), *The Development of Standard English 1300–1800* (Cambridge: Cambridge University Press, 2000).

Index

AB language 38–9, 51, 137–8
accent 6, 8, 33–4, 37, 47–9, 63, 83, 130–1
affixation 81, 89–90
agreement 106, 114
Ælfric 11–2, 35, 138
allophone 52, 61
American English 54, 71
analogy 62, 65, 113, 114, 130
Ancrene Wisse/Riwle 15–16, 19, 38–9, 46, 138
Anglian 11, 122
Anglo-Norman 20–2
Auchinleck manuscript 40
aureate diction 88
Ayenbite of Inwyt 17–19, 138

Bede 11, 12, 13, 36
borrowing 53, 75, 78, 82–95, 129, 141

Cædmon's *Hymn* 12–13
Capgrave, John 26–8
Caxton, William 34, 42–3, 49, 68
Celtic 10–1, 84–5, 89
Central Midlands Standard 40, 140
Chancery Standard 44–5, 51, 134, 139–40

Chaucer, Geoffrey 22–5, 37, 40–3, 48, 79, 92, 98, 100, 115, 124–5, 133, 139, 141–2
Cheke, Sir John 65–6, 92
colourless usage 44–5
compounding 74–6, 81–2, 89–90
contact 61, 82, 83, 85, 86, 95, 97, 100–1, 119, 124
conversion 74–6, 81, 90

determiners 23, 106, 112–14, 129
digraphs 56–7, 67

East Anglian 28, 40, 62
Ellesmere manuscript 24–5, 40–2, 145
etymology 3, 63–4, 66, 90, 94–5,

fit-technique 22–3

Gawain-poet 22, 37, 129, 132
Gower, John 22, 24, 26, 41–3, 141
grapheme 52–4, 60–1, 67

h-dropping 1, 6, 62
Hart, John 30, 49, 66–7
Hengwrt manuscript 24–5, 40–2, 145
holograph 17–18, 22, 26–7, 31

homophony 30, 100–1, 111
hypercorrection 8, 38

inflexions 4–5, 14, 73–4, 105–20
inkhorn terms 93–4

Johnson, Samuel 43, 69–70, 91

Labov, William 7–9
Laȝamon 16, 19, 86, 138
Langland, William 22, 24, 37, 41, 139, 141
Lindisfarne Gospels gloss 56, 110
Linguistic Atlas of Late ME 23–4, 39, 137–9
literatim copying 17, 22, 24, 38
Lydgate, John 88

manuscripts 11, 16–29, 36–43, 66, 136–40
Mercian 11–2, 36, 113
Michel, Dan 18–9, 138
mischsprache 17
Mulcaster, Richard 49, 67–9, 94

neologisms 92
Northumbrian 11–14, 110, 113

Ormulum 16–9, 86, 114, 133
Owl and Nightingale 16–17, 20, 39, 77, 121

palaeography 24–5, 41–2
Paston letters 28, 31, 45–6, 127, 139–40
phonaesthesia 102
Pinkhurst, Adam 25–6
place names 11, 85, 130
prescriptivism 6–9, 29–10, 32, 62, 70
prestige 5–6, 33, 44, 124
printing 28–9, 42–3, 47, 69, 71, 136
pronouns 23, 75, 86, 101, 110–14, 120–34
Puttenham, George 49, 94

received pronunciation 6, 33–4
runes 14, 54–6, 57, 59

scribes 10, 15–17, 20, 22–6, 36–8, 40–2, 115, 136–9
semantic change 2, 95–103, 142
Shakespeare, William 51, 64, 80–2, 93–4, 98, 111, 118–9, 126, 131
Smith, Sir Thomas 66, 120
spelling reform 29, 63–71, 120
standardization 5–6, 33–51
subjunctive 116–18

West Saxon 11, 35, 51, 136–7

CPSIA information can be obtained
at www.ICGtesting.com
Printed in the USA
LVHW081522311218
602287LV00020B/1536/P